Music in Ireland

Music in Ireland

∞

EXPERIENCING MUSIC,
EXPRESSING CULTURE

∞

DOROTHEA E. HAST
STANLEY SCOTT

New York   Oxford
Oxford University Press
2004

Oxford University Press

Oxford New York
Auckland Bangkok Buenos Aires Cape Town Chennai
Dar es Salaam Delhi Hong Kong Istanbul Karachi Kolkata
Kuala Lumpur Madrid Melbourne Mexico City Mumbai
Nairobi São Paulo Shanghai Taipei Tokyo Toronto

Published by Oxford University Press, Inc.
198 Madison Avenue, New York, New York, 10016
www.oup.com

Oxford is a registered trademark of Oxford University Press

Library of Congress Cataloging-in-Publication Data
Hast, Dorothea E.
    Music in Ireland : experiencing music, expressing culture / Dorothea E. Hast,
Stanley Scott.
        p. cm.—(Global music series)
    Includes bibliographical references (p.) and index.
    ISBN 0-19-514555-0 (pbk. : alk. paper) — ISBN-13 978-0-19-514555-7
        1. Folk music—Ireland—History and criticism. I. Scott, Stan (Stanley Arnold)
    II. Title. III. Series.

ML3654.H35 2004
781.62'91620415—dc22

                                                                        2003065467

Printing number: 9 8 7

Printed in the United States of America
on acid-free paper

GLOBAL MUSIC SERIES

General Editors: Bonnie C. Wade and Patricia Shehan Campbell

Music in East Africa, Gregory Barz
Music in Central Java, Benjamin Brinner
Teaching Music Globally, Patricia Shehan Campbell
Carnival Music in Trinidad, Shannon Dudley
Music in Bali, Lisa Gold
Music in Ireland, Dorothea E. Hast and Stanley Scott
Music in the Middle East, Scott Marcus
Music in Brazil, John Patrick Murphy
Music in America, Adelaide Reyes
Music in Bulgaria, Timothy Rice
Music in North India, George E. Ruckert
Mariachi Music in America, Daniel Sheehy
Music in West Africa, Ruth M. Stone
Music in South India, T. Viswanathan and Matthew Harp Allen
Music in Japan, Bonnie C. Wade
Thinking Musically, Bonnie C. Wade
Music in China, J. Lawrence Witzleben

Contents

∞

Foreword

In the past three decades interest in music around the world has surged, as evidenced in the proliferation of courses at the college level, the burgeoning "world music" market in the recording business, and the extent to which musical performance is evoked as a lure in the international tourist industry. This heightened interest has encouraged an explosion in ethnomusicological research and publication, including the production of reference works and textbooks. The original model for the "world music" course—if this is Tuesday, this must be Japan—has grown old, as has the format of textbooks for it, either a series of articles in single multiauthored volumes that subscribe to the idea of "a survey" and have created a canon of cultures for study, or single-authored studies purporting to cover world musics or ethnomusicology. The time has come for a change.

This Global Music Series offers a new paradigm. Teachers can now design their own courses; choosing from a set of case study volumes, they can decide which and how many musics they will cover. The series also does something else; rather than uniformly taking a large region and giving superficial examples from several different countries within it, in some case studies authors have focused on a specific culture or a few countries within a larger region. Its length and approach permits each volume greater depth than the usual survey. Themes significant in each volume guide the choice of music that is discussed. The contemporary musical situation is the point of departure in all the volumes, with historical information and traditions covered as they elucidate the present. In addition, a set of unifying topics such as gender, globalization, and authenticity occur throughout the series. These are addressed in the framing volume, *Thinking Musically*, which sets the stage for the case studies by introducing ways to think about how people make music meaningful and useful in their lives and presenting basic musical concepts as they are practiced in musical systems around the world. A second framing volume, *Teaching Music Globally*, guides teachers in the use of *Thinking Musically* and the case studies.

The series subtitle, "Experiencing Music, Expressing Culture," also puts in the forefront the people who make music or in some other way experience it and also through it express shared culture. This resonance with global history studies, with their focus on processes and themes that permit cross-study, occasions the title of this Global Music Series.

Bonnie C. Wade
Patricia Shehan Campbell
General Editors

Preface

This short volume focuses on Irish traditional music—forms of singing, instrumental music, and dance that are closely interwoven with Ireland's rich cultural history. The music thrives today not only in Ireland, but in pockets throughout North America, Europe, Australia, and Asia. Because we cannot document the whole of this vital living tradition, most of our discussion is centered on individuals and communities in Ireland, particularly in Clare, Dublin, and Armagh. We introduce themes, contexts, and music through the eyes, voices, and instruments of a few representative musicians and scholars, in order to emphasize the importance of people and places in music making, as well as to illuminate larger national and international trends. In the interest of brevity we have highlighted certain areas and musicians while omitting others. We hope that this brief introduction will lead the reader to explore further and discover some of the wonderful musicians who could not be included in these pages.

The complexities and ambiguities of the word "tradition" fuel our discussion throughout this book as we examine the performance and transmission of Irish traditional music. Music-making today reveals continuities with the not-so-distant past, when music was an essential component of community life. In Chapters 1–5, we focus on this ongoing dialectic between past and present, while in Chapter 6, we introduce issues of commercialism, globalization, and cross cultural collaboration. Many artists have entered the global marketplace today through recordings, tours, and large-scale productions such as *Riverdance*, and as a result, new meanings, terms, styles, and fusions have emerged from the commodification of traditional genres.

Our own journey into Irish music began in the 1970s, when a new generation of young Irish musicians discovered and embraced what had seemed, only a few years earlier, a waning musical tradition. The recordings and concerts of groups such as Planxty, the Boys of the Lough, and the Bothy Band were infused with a vibrant energy that quickly drew the attention of young American folk musicians, including ourselves. It was a small step to begin adding Irish songs and tunes to our American repertoire (already partly Irish in its roots). This modest beginning led to our first "collecting" expeditions to Ireland in 1984 and 1985. Our focus on the acquisition of repertoire rapidly broadened to a study of the music culture as a whole, as we discovered that understanding the music would require us to understand the context which gave it meaning. Subsequent trips focused on both performance and ethnomusicological research; our last research trip was in 2001, when we recorded many of the interviews and performances that contributed to the creation of this project.

ACKNOWLEDGMENTS

This book has been a collaborative process from the beginning. We have been helped at every stage by music lovers who shared their time, expertise, and enthusiasm with us. Our writing would not have been possible without their generosity and hospitality. We would like to begin by thanking the Camerons of Purbeck Lodge, Monkstown, who have provided us with a home away from home ever since our first trip to Ireland. They have supplied us with many wonderful meals, evenings of wine and song, and our first essential introductions to Dublin's musical world.

We must next thank our friends in Miltown Malbay, County Clare. Tom and Annette Munnelly have furnished us with countless meals, cups of tea, a great deal of fun, and enormous insight into the local music culture. Tom has also given us formal interviews, detailed critiques of this book, and access to his own extensive research and recordings. We are most grateful to Paddy Galvin and his family, Muiris and Úna Uí Rócháin, Kitty Hayes for a great afternoon of music and conversation in her home, and Nell and Jimmy Gleeson for their interview and always welcoming hospitality at Gleesons Pub. In addition, we would like to thank Tim Dennehy for his contribution to our CD, Peter Laban for his wonderful photographs, and Brid O'Donohue for a wealth of tunes and musical insight.

Many other generous people consented to be interviewed and invariably these interviews led to hours of conversation, cups of tea, and a meal. We would especially like to acknowledge the help of Jerry O'Reilly, including his recording that appears on our CD. His energy and enthusiasm animated many of the singing sessions and set dances that we have attended throughout Ireland. We would also like to thank Desi Wilkinson for putting us up in Limerick and giving us a great interview and a few tunes in his sunny kitchen. His insight as both performer and scholar are greatly appreciated. Len Graham and Pádraigín Ní Uallacháin made a special trip down to Dublin to be interviewed and recorded, and have been especially generous with their contributions to our book and CD. Mary MacNamara took us into her home and gave unstintingly of her time and expertise. We would also like to thank Jerry O'Sullivan, Brian O'Rourke, Tomás Ó Canainn, Mel Mercier, Joe Gerhard, Niall Vallely, Ashley Sheridan, Wendy Newton, and Danny Gardella for their help with this project.

We would also like to acknowledge the many musicians who contributed recordings for our CD. We would like to start by thanking Mícheál Ó Súilleabháin, along with Sandra Joyce, for making a special recording of "The Old Grey Goose." We would also like to thank Andy Irvine for his time and generosity in helping us to include his recording of "Edward Connors." Kevin Crawford and Cillian Vallely both provided us with wonderful interviews, and then went out of their way to help us make a recording of their group Lúnasa at the Towne Crier Café in Amenia, New York. We are most grateful to them, along with their fellow band members, Seán Smyth, Donogh Hennessy, and Trevor Hutchinson, and to Towne Crier owner Phil Ciganer. Special thanks go to Michael Tubridy, Eamon McGivney, and to the memory of Junior Crehan and Tommy McCarthy for their wonderful playing on the first recorded selection. We also wish to thank our playing partners Sally Perreten and George Wilson for their recorded contributions.

We must also acknowledge the many people who helped us obtain recordings, lyrics, and photographs. Special thanks go to Larry Lynch, Harry Bradshaw, Sean Williams, Terry Moylan, Jody Cormack, Ted McGraw, Ita Crehan, Nicky McAuliffe, Nicholas Carolan at the Traditional Music Archive, Laurel Sercombe at the University of Washington Ethnomusicology Archives, and Beth Sweeney at the Irish Music Center of Boston College. We are also grateful to the Department of Irish Folklore at University College Dublin, The National Gallery of Ireland, Appletree Press, Connoisseur Music, Romophone Records, and Gael-linn Records.

We wish to thank James Cowdery, Mick Moloney, and other readers of this text for their detailed critiques. Thanks also to our educational consultant Marie McCarthy, and to all our editors, including series coeditor Pat Campbell, and Jan Beatty, Talia Krohn, and Lisa Grzan at Oxford University Press. We would especially like to express our gratitude to series coeditor Bonnie Wade, who invited us to write this book and gave us generous support and critical commentary throughout the writing process.

Pronunciation Guide

In many cases, the pronunciation of Irish words is not obvious from the spelling. Several letters are left out of the Irish alphabet (j, q, v, w, x, and z) and many combinations of vowels and consonants are sounded quite differently from their appearance on the page. Each vowel has a long value (written with an accent or *fada*) and a short value, while each consonant has a slender and broad value. A consonant is slender if it is preceded by i or e and broad if it is preceded by a, o, or u. In addition, the three main regions of the Irish *Gaeltacht* (Irish speaking areas) have their own dialects. The following guide is a brief introduction to a few of the common sounds.

á: pronounced *aw* (*Pádraigín:* Pawdrageen)

é: pronounced *ay* as in say (*Éireann:* Ayrinn)

í: pronounced *ee* (*sí:* she)

ó: pronounced *oh*

ú: pronounced *oo* as in fool (*Cúchulainn:* Koochullin)

s (slender): pronounced like the English *sh* (*Séan:* Shawn; *feis:* fesh; *aisling:* ashling)

c: at beginning of word, pronounced *k* as in cane (*céilí:* kaylee)

th: pronounced as *h* (*máthair* sounds like mawhir)

bh: pronounced as *v* (*sliabh:* shleeav)

adh: at end of word, pronounced *ah* (*fleadh:* flah)

ch (broad): sounds like "ch" in Bach or the Scottish loch

comh: at beginning of word, pronounced *ko* (*Comhaltas:* Koltas)

CD Track List

1. Junior Crehan (fiddle), Michael Tubridy (flute), Tommy McCarthy (concertina), and Eamon McGivney (fiddle), "The Maid Behind the Bar/Gregg's Pipes" (reels). *Set Dances of Ireland, Volume 1*, Séadna 001. 1992. Produced by Larry Lynch. larrylynch@sanbrunocable. com. 650/588-9969. Permission given by Larry Lynch.

2. Tim Dennehy, "Farewell to Miltown Malbay," *Farewell to Miltown Malbay*. Sceilig Records, Mullach, County Clare, Ireland. 1997. Permission given by Tim Dennehy.

3. Kitty Hayes (concertina), "Mist Covered Mountain" (J. Crehan) and "Tommy Whelan's" (jigs). Recorded at her home by the authors. Permission given by Kitty Hayes. Permission to use "The Mist Covered Mountain" composed by Junior Crehan courtesy of Connoisseur Music, Ireland.

4. Dublin Metropolitan Garda Céilí Band, "The Sunshine/Humors of Castle Bernard/Dick Sands" (hornpipes). *The Great Céilí Bands Volume 1*, remastered by Ted McGraw, notes by Séamus MacMathúna and Ted McGraw. Published by Comhaltas Ceoltóirí Éireann. Medley originally issued by HMV IM331 (1937) on a 78 LPM. Permission given by Ted McGraw. mcgraw@netacc.net

5. Sally Perreten (harp), "Planxty Johnson" by Turlough Carolan, recorded by the authors at her home. Permission given by Sally Perreten.

6. John McCormack,"The Harp That Once Through Tara's Halls" by Thomas Moore. Remastered on *John McCormack: the acoustic Victor and HMV recordings (1912–14)*. Romophone Records, 1997. Permission given by Romophone Records.

7. Joe Heaney, "The Rocks of Bawn" from *Say A Song: Joe Heaney in the Pacific Northwest*. Northwest Folklife and the University of Wash-

ington Ethnomusicology Archives, 1996. Permission given from Northwest Folklife and the Joe Heaney Collection of the University of Washington Ethnomusicology Archives. Special thanks to Laurel Sercombe.

8. Andy Irvine, "Edward Connors" from *Rainy Sundays . . . Windy Dreams*. CD TÜT 72.141, with Andy Irvine (vocals and Fylde bouzouki), Donal Lunny (harmonium and guitar), and Frankie Gavin (fiddle). Wundertüte Musik, 1989. Permission given by Andy Irvine and Wundertüte Records. www.Andyirvine.com.

9. Michael Coleman (fiddle) and Herbert G. Henry (piano), "Dr Gilbert/The Queen of May" (reels). Remastered and released on *Michael Coleman 1891–1945*. CEFCD 161. Gael-Linn and Viva Voce 1992. Produced by Harry Bradshaw. Originally issued by Columbia 33375-F, W110796-2 (1929). Permission given by Sony Music and Harry Bradshaw.

10. Mary MacNamara (concertina), "The Ash Plant/The Dog Among the Bushes" (reels), recorded by the authors at her home. Permission given by Mary MacNamara.

11. Demonstration of ornaments: ornament 1: cut; ornament 2: short roll; ornament 3: long roll; ornament 4: triplet; ornament 5: cran; played on tin whistle by Dorothea Hast.

12. Stan Scott (mandolin), "The Road to Lisdoonvarna" (demonstration of a single jig).

13. Stan Scott (mandolin) and Dorothea Hast (tin whistle), "A Fig for a Kiss" (demonstration of a slip jig).

14. Stan Scott (mandolin), "O'Keefe's Slide" (demonstration of a slide).

15. Kevin Crawford (flute), "The Reel of Rio/The Woman of the House" (reels), recorded by the authors at his home. Permission given by Kevin Crawford.

16. Kitchen Céilí (George Wilson, fiddle, Dorothea Hast, tin whistle, and Stan Scott, guitar), Two Kerry polkas. Permission given by authors.

17. Kitchen Céilí (fiddle, tenor recorder, and guitar), "Planxty Fanny Powers" (waltz) by Turlough Carolan. Permission given by authors.

18. Jerry O'Sullivan, "Garrett Barry's Jig" (first version). Recorded by authors in Yonkers, New York. Permission given by Jerry O'Sullivan.

19. Jerry O'Sullivan, "Garrett Barry's Jig" (second version). Recorded by authors in Yonkers, New York. Permission given by Jerry O'Sullivan.

20. Tom Lenihan, "The Blarney Stone" from *The Mt. Callan Garland: Songs from the Repertoire of Tom Lenihan*. Collected and edited by Tom Munnelly. *Comhairle Bhéaloideas Éireann*, 1994. Permission given from The Head of Department, Department of Irish Folklore, University College Dublin on behalf of *Comhairle Bhéaloideas Éireann*.

21. Jerry O'Reilly, "The Carmagnole." Recorded by the authors in Ennistymon. Permission given by Jerry O'Reilly.

22. Joe Heaney,"Lament of the Three Marys" from *Say A Song: Joe Heaney in the Pacific Northwest*. Northwest Folklife and the University of Washington Ethnomusicology Archives, 1996. Permission from Northwest Folklife and the Joe Heaney Collection at the University of Washington Ethnomusicology Archives.

23. Pádraigín Ní Uallacháin, "Úirchill a' Chreagáin" (Creggan Graveyard). Gael-linn CEFCD 174. Permission given by Pádraigín Ní Uallacháin. www.irishsong.com

24. Len Graham, "Love Won't You Marry Me." Recorded by authors in Dublin. Permission given by Len Graham. www.irishsong.com

25. Len Graham, "Banks of the Bann" (first version). Recorded by authors in Dublin. Permission given by Len Graham.

26. Len Graham, "Banks of the Bann" (second version). Recorded by authors in Dublin. Permission given by Len Graham.

27. Mícheál Ó Súilleabháin, "The Old Grey Goose." Live performance at the Irish World Music Centre, University of Limerick, September 2003. With Mícheál Ó Súilleabháin (piano) and Sandra Joyce *(bodhrán)*. Permission given by Mícheál Ó Súilleabháin.

28. Lúnasa, "Dr. Gilbert/Merry Sisters of Fate/Longacre" (reels) recorded live at the Town Crier Café in Pawling, New York, July 25, 2003. Permission given by Phil Ciganer at the Town Crier Café, Pawling, New York and Kevin Crawford. www.lunasa.ie.

CHAPTER 1

Invitation to a Session

"Listen, Stan and Dora. There will be music, dancing, and singing tonight at Gleesons Pub in Coore. Here's how you get there." Jerry O'Reilly leans over our table and draws a small map, providing directions for a twelve-mile drive along the western Irish coast and then inland on narrow, hedged country roads. We are sitting in a small restaurant in the coastal town of Ennistymon in County Clare, where dozens of singers from Ireland and abroad have gathered for a weekend festival of traditional singing. It is Sunday evening, and the festival has begun to wind down as weekenders return to their homes.

Jerry's manner seems almost conspiratorial, as he moves between tables, inviting a handful of friends to the session. He speaks quietly and efficiently, as if sharing a secret only with those who "need to know." Gleesons has hosted music, singing, and dancing on Sunday nights for four generations in the small farming hamlet of Coore. While festivals, schools, clubs, competitions, and concert halls provide important venues for the sharing of Irish traditional music today, these are, by definition, *contrived* occasions, created by people who set out to promote the tradition. Gleesons provides a different kind of experience: the life of the music in a community where the music has been getting along "on its own," patronized by local people and performed by local musicians, for generations. Jerry's approach is therefore both welcoming and protective, wanting to share this unusual session with outsiders who will be able to appreciate and participate in it, but wary of drawing in people who would not respect the sensitive cultural ecology of this local tradition.

We, Dora Hast and Stan Scott, are outsiders here, American musicians with a long-standing passion for Irish traditional music. Jerry's invitation on this night in early June, 1997 is a pleasant surprise. At half-past nine we set out, following Jerry's directions down the coast and then inland for a few miles. The sun will not set for another hour, and

1

the Atlantic sparkles to the west, while the verdant hills of West Clare roll gently to the east. The narrow roads grow narrower still as we approach Coore. We dip and bounce over a short bridge and find ourselves before two whitewashed buildings, a two-story farmhouse attached to a long, low pub with the words "Gleesons" and "Coore" printed above the door.

We find a parking place among a dozen cars, and enter the pub. The front door opens into a small passageway with doors leading into a single, spacious room. Entering, we find ourselves facing a side wall with a large fireplace. Before the fireplace stand two tables, where a number of older patrons sit talking. In the back corner fits a small stage with four empty chairs, an accordion, and several fiddle cases poised where their players have left them. Photographs of musicians adorn the wall to the left of the stage; also displayed are poems by Junior (Martin) Crehan, the eighty-nine-year-old fiddler who has led these Sunday night sessions for more than fifty years. The remainder of the long back wall is taken up by the bar, where the pub owners, Jim and Nell Gleeson and their sons and daughters, serve drinks. Before the left-hand wall stands a second bar, behind which various foodstuffs are displayed on shelves. In the not-too-distant past, many country pubs served as grocery stores and post offices as well as taverns. While Jimmy and Nell continue the grocery tradition today, they have far fewer customers since their local post office was closed.

We move to the bar where we are greeted by a number of regular attenders of the session. Some were born within a mile of the pub, and have danced to the music of Junior Crehan all their lives. Others have moved to the area from Dublin, London, or the United States, drawn by the rich musical traditions of West Clare. Some are expatriated Irish, who return home from places like New York, Boston, London, and Manchester during their summer holidays. Local patrons of Gleesons include farmers (like the Gleesons themselves, and many of the musicians who have played in the pub over the years), old age pensioners (fifty to sixty of them in the nearby hills), teachers (like Muiris Ó Rócháin and Harry Hughes, who run the famous Willie Clancy School of traditional music each July), and folklorists (like Tom Munnelly, director of the Ennistymon Singing Festival).

After a few minutes, the musicians move to the stage. Junior Crehan and Michael Downes are the senior fiddlers, each in his eighties. Kitty Hayes, whose late husband Josie played flute with Junior for seven decades, plays concertina. Eamon McGivney, fiddler, and Conor Keane, accordionist, represent a younger generation of players steeped in the

FIGURE 1.1 *Nell Gleeson.* *(Photo by Dorothea Hast)*

music of West Clare. Peter Laban (tin whistle and bagpipes) and Gabi and Geoff Wooff (fiddle and concertina), European and British expatriates who live nearby, complete the ensemble. Drawn to Clare by their love of the music, they have become permanent residents of the area and frequent players at Gleesons.

They begin their set with a gentle, lilting jig, "The Mist Covered Mountain," composed by Junior Crehan. He has composed some forty tunes, many of which have entered the traditional repertoire (Munnelly, 70). Every few minutes, the musicians switch to a new tune, moving seamlessly from one melody to the next. Finishing their first set of jigs, the musicians chat together and refresh themselves with the drinks that Nell Gleeson has placed beside each player: pints of Guinness stout, or glasses of soda water with lemon and a cherry. Their thirsts temporarily quenched, the players launch into a set of reels.

The music is only lightly amplified; "anchor" players, Junior, Eamon, and Conor, play into microphones, but the music is purposefully kept down to a level that allows patrons at the bar to carry on conversations. As pub owner Jimmy Gleeson explains:

> People that come in there want to come in and converse and talk and maybe sell a bullock or a heifer or something like that among themselves. It's a farming community. So it's very important that you can hold a conversation, listen to the music if you want to. If someone is

FIGURE 1.2 *Jimmy Gleeson.* *(Photo by Dorothea Hast)*

singing then, that's the one time, the only thing I want to hear when someone is singing is the big clock ticking. And you know when you can hear the clock ticking that you have silence (J. Gleeson in discussion with authors).

For some time, we talk with friends as the musicians continue to play, sip their drinks, and converse with each other. Their playing is neither a performance in the conventional sense nor background music. Instead, they are a complete unit within themselves—playing for each other and immensely enjoying one another's company. Three of the musicians sit offstage facing the other musicians, with their backs to the pub patrons. They make no announcements to the crowd, but joke with each other, enjoying the *craic* (chat, pronounced "crack") as they take leisurely pauses between sets of tunes. Their own self-involvement makes no demands on the patrons, but their presence and music enliven and enrich the whole atmosphere of the pub.

Then several dancers appear on the open floor in front of the stage; one of them asks Junior to provide music for the "Caledonian Set." Conversation is reduced to a murmur, as all eyes move to the dance floor. The musicians launch into a fast reel for the first section of this traditional set dance, and four couples begin moving gracefully through the figures, stepping in time to the music. This dance is one in a genre of social dances performed in square formation that were first brought to Ireland by French dancing masters in the mid-to-late nineteenth century. Originally called "Sets of Quadrilles," the dances were also exported from France to England and the United States. The dances were quickly indigenized in Ireland by the composition of new choreography and the use of Irish dance tunes for the accompanying music. While set dances have enjoyed a remarkable revival all over Ireland during the last twenty years, some areas such as Coore have had an almost unbroken tradition of set dancing since the genre was first introduced. Many regions have their own localized set, and in West Clare, it is the Caledonian.

ACTIVITY 1.1 *Listen to the dance music of Junior Crehan (fiddle), Michael Tubridy (flute), Tommy McCarthy (concertina), and Eamon McGivney (fiddle) on CD track 1. They recorded these two reels, "The Maid Behind the Bar" and "Gregg's Pipes," in 1992. To learn more about the Caledonian Set, including how to dance the first figure, please go to our website, www.oup.com/us/globalmusic.*

FIGURE 1.3   *Dancing the Caledonian Set in Gleesons.*   *(Photo © Peter Laban, Miltown Malbay, County Clare, Ireland)*

During the relative lull in conversation, the music seems sweeter and more compelling. The dancers conclude their set, conversation resumes, and the musicians begin a new set of reels. Before being drawn into a new conversation, I (Stan Scott) decide to move closer to the stage, where I will be able to concentrate on the music. I am gradually drawn in by the flowing rhythm and subtle ornaments of the players, who themselves seem to have entered a state of trance-like concentration. For some time, perhaps ten or fifteen minutes, I am swept along by the music, hypnotized by its charm. Then the players stop, stand, place their instruments on their chairs, stretch, and move to the floor for an interval of conversation with friends. Junior Crehan greets me and shakes my hand.

"Do you like the music?" he asks me.

"It's beautiful music," I reply.

"Did you ever hear Willie Clancy play the pipes?" he asks.

"Only on recordings."

"He was a mighty player. I wrote a poem about him:

I am writing those lines with tears in my eyes
For a comrade who now has departed
And my soul is heavy with grief and woe
And I'm almost broken-hearted,
For the voice of the one that we'll surely miss
A voice that is gone forever
Oh! Willie asthore we'll see you no more
Oh! never, never, never.

There's a gap in tradition that ne'er will be filled
A wide gap that ne'er shall be mended
On the hill o'er the town we laid you down
'Twas sad that your young life ended.

FIGURE 1.4 *Junior Crehan.* *(Photo © Peter Laban, Miltown Malbay, County Clare, Ireland)*

Let's hope that we'll meet in that brighter land
  With music and song for ever
Aroon aroon you were taken too soon
  And your music we'll hear again never.

You are up in high Heaven I hope tonight
  With your father and mother who bore you
And the Dorans and Rowsome and Scully and Tadg
  The musicians who went before you
By night and by day for you I will pray
  To the Blessed God above you
That His Angels may gather you under their wings
  Is the prayer of one who loved you. " (Crehan 1973)

In this tribute, which Junior composed in 1973, the year of Willie Clancy's death, Junior honors an old friend and playing partner, and also pays homage to the preceding generation of players who moved through the area, pipers and fiddlers who passed the music on to Willie Clancy and Junior Crehan. As he speaks into my ear above the din of pub conversation, I am flattered to be the solitary audience of his recitation, but we will later discover that this personal, welcoming demeanor—and conversational virtuosity—was typical of Junior throughout his life. Jimmy Gleeson recalls that back in the early days,

> there was a kind of routine. They were very gentle modest people who would come in the door quietly with their instruments usually hanging down by their legs, like they were sneaking it in, and they would park their instruments somewhere around the stage, if you had a stage. A lot of places only had a big table or something like that and they'd stick them under the table. And they would drink a few pints first and chat and the conversation was often as interesting as the music. Junior was a great storyteller and a great entertainer in that light. He'd circulate and meet all the people (J. Gleeson in discussion with authors, June 2001)

Junior Crehan was an example par excellence of the holistic nature of Irish performance traditions: a musician, composer, storyteller, and dancer—who sometimes danced steps while playing the fiddle!

After the musicians have spent a few minutes mixing with friends at the bar, a solo voice rises with the first few notes of a song. Half a dozen tongues "shush" the crowd. Tim Dennehy is the singer; he moved from Dublin to Miltown Malbay in West Clare some two decades back, drawn, like so many, by music. A founder of Dublin's *Góilín* Singer's

Club, he now broadcasts programs of traditional music for Clare FM, a local radio station based in the nearby town of Ennis. He frequently sings *sean-nós* songs, "old-style" repertoire in Irish Gaelic, but on this occasion he chooses to sing an English-language song:

> *Farewell to Miltown Malbay, a long and sad farewell,*
> *The sorrow in my heart today no words of mine can tell.*
> *I'm parting from my dear old friends, the scenes I fondly love,*
> *May happiness attend them all, and blessings from above . . .*

(CD track 2: Tim Dennehy singing "Farewell to Miltown Malbay.")

Tim continues his solo, unaccompanied performance through seven verses written by Miltown Malbay poet Tomás Ó hAodha (1866–1935). The song praises the beauty of the West Clare landscape, the kind hearts of the people who live there, and local cultural traditions, including the bagpiping of Garrett Barry—cousin of Junior Crehan's grandmother,

FIGURE 1.5   *Tim Dennehy.*   *(Photo used with permission by Tim Dennehy. Photographer: Michael Killeen, Killeen Photography, Miltown Malbay, County Clare.)*

from the generation just preceding "the Dorans and Rowsome" eulo-
gized in Junior's tribute to Willie Clancy. In songs, poetry, storytelling
and conversation, a powerful vein of praise for places and people (particularly musicians), runs through the culture of Irish traditional music,
providing motivation to pass songs, music, and stories on to future generations. Songs and dance tunes are so frequently linked to particular
singers, players, places and events that every step one takes towards
the music (as a singer, player, dancer, or listener) seems to envelop one
further among the threads of the culture that surrounds it.

As the night continues, more songs are heard in both Irish and English, more jigs and reels are played, another set is danced, and, perhaps, some heifers and bullocks are bought and sold. The musicians finally stop playing around 1 o'clock in the morning and the patrons
gradually begin leaving for home. What is the history behind these Sunday night sessions in Coore? How did Junior Crehan become such a
central figure in these sessions?

When Junior Crehan was born in 1908, Gleesons was a smaller establishment—a small pub in the farmhouse kitchen. Jimmy and Nell are
now the fourth generation of Gleesons to run the pub. Jimmy recalls
that even in his grandfather's day,

> there was always music. It was never an organized thing. Every house
> nearly had some kind of an instrument, mostly back then a fiddle or
> a concertina. The concert flute and the tin whistle came in later on
> and there was no such thing as a guitar back then. You might get an
> occasional banjo, but it was mostly concertina—concertinas were very
> popular (ibid).

ACTIVITY 1.2   *Listen to CD track 3 to hear the sound of
the concertina played solo by Kitty Hayes. She performs two jigs,
beginning with Junior Crehan's tune "The Mist Covered Mountain" followed by "Tommy Whelan's Jig."*

During Junior Crehan's childhood, dances accompanied by fiddle
and concertina were regular outdoor events at crossroads like
Markham's Cross, one mile from Junior's home. Music and dancing also
took place on Sunday evenings at the Lenihan household in nearby
Knockbrack. The Lenihans always had the latest 78 rpm recordings of

Irish music from America; Junior would borrow one record each week, take it home, learn the tunes, and exchange it for a new record the following Sunday. Junior's first instrument was the concertina, which he began learning from his mother at age six. Junior's first fiddle teacher was an itinerant dancing master and fiddler named Thady Casey; by the age of twelve, Junior and flutist Josie Hayes were playing music in Gleeson's kitchen. Junior's storytelling mentor was Pat Murrihey, who conveyed in English the stories his own father had told in Irish Gaelic. The three generations, from the elder Murrihey to Pat to Junior, represent the transition of West Clare from an Irish-speaking to an English-speaking environment (Munnelly 1998, 64–5).

As a young man, Junior attended college for a short time, but was delighted to return home to work his family's farm—and to play the fiddle. His father, Martin Crehan Senior (1876–1973), a schoolteacher and farmer, did not approve of music and dancing. Folklorist Tom Munnelly writes:

> Living at home meant having to cope with his loving but austere father, and there was continual conflict between Junior's growing fondness for music and dance and the demands of running a farm efficiently. Many times Junior would be out all night at a house dance and in order to impress his father would have to try and look bright and breezy to avoid detection. He took to hiding his pyjamas in the barn and when he returned at dawn he would put them on, conceal his fiddle where he had hidden the pyjamas and enter the house carrying a pot in his hand so that his father would think he had just been out to feed the hens! (ibid., 64).

Another of Junior's teachers was itinerant dancing master and fiddler Paddy Barron, an older rival of Thady Casey who taught step and set dancing in local homes. The step dances are virtuosic solo dances based on the hornpipe, reel, and jig, in which the dancer's foot movements create percussive patterns on the floor, while the sets are group figure dances in square formation. Junior accompanied Barron's classes in the 1930s. Getting tunes from the dance master was not always easy. Junior asked to learn a tune called "The Drunken Gauger," but Barron was reluctant to teach it. Junior finally arranged to learn it secretly, by eavesdropping in the home of one of his friends. In Junior's own words:

> "Come early to my house," the man of the house said, "on Sunday evening, and have your fiddle tuned and I'll question him about it."

I already had the first part of the tune in spite of Barron, but I couldn't get the long part. I couldn't think of it. So:
"Stay in the porch," says your man.
So I did, and I had the fiddle ready. He went in to Barron.
"Barron," he said, "I didn't hear you playing 'The Drunken Gauger' with forty years."
"Yerra", he said, "I don't care about it. 'Tisn't much good."
"Play it till I hear it."
So he played it. And I was in the porch and I picking up the notes. And your man says to him—
"I thought 'twas different to that," says he. "Play it again," says he.
So he played it again.
"Begod, I don't know. I thought there was more in it than that."
He played it four or five times. He played it around three times and stopped and your man put him on again and he played it maybe four times. By the time he was done I had it. And I was the only one that kept it (ibid., 83).

In this tradition where musicians learn by oral transmission, tunes have often been regarded as the personal property of the musicians who played them. While most musicians have been generous in sharing their repertory, it was sometimes necessary to learn by stealth, especially before the widespread use of the tape recorder and the growth of the recording industry.

On one occasion, Junior attributed the persuasive charm of his music to a gift from the fairies. He had finished playing for the dancing at one house party, where he had been rewarded with food and a good deal of drink, and was walking at midnight to another house to play for a second party:

I had to come back by this fairy rath [ring fort—an ancient earthen rampart]. It was on the side of a hill and there was a level field to the right of it and you would never see it until you come on top of the step on the stile that was leading to it. The moon was out and the odd cloud would go across the moon and she would get dark for a while and then get bright again. There was a hedge down by the southern side of the rath and you would never see it until you come up a bit in the field. As I was coming along I stood on the stile and I saw this little ball of light going to and fro. It would shine very bright and when it would come on to the ground it would get dark. So I came off the stile anyway, and as I was walking didn't I see two goal posts and a little man standing in between the goal posts? and the ball was coming!

"Stop the ball," says he.

I stopped the ball and I put my leg on it. It hit me on the side of the ankle.

"A good job for me," says he, "that you did it" (ibid., 110).

Junior observed the playing of two teams of little men, one team in red, the other in green, until the cock crowed and all but the goaltender disappeared. Junior walked on with the little man, who spoke mixed Irish and English and came up only to Junior's knee. The goaltender, who was a rush-fairy, gave Junior a piece of metal "about half the size of a horseshoe nail" to put behind the bridge of his fiddle, as a charm to win a wife. Proceeding to his next engagement, Junior saw that the girl he admired, Cissy Walsh, was among the dancers:

They put her up step dancing. She did not live very far from myself. I used to see her working and she was well able. But anyway that night I put my yoke of a charm on the string of the fiddle. She was dancing a reel. And the reel I was playing, I'll never forget it, the name of it was "The Girl That Broke My Heart."

While the music was on the people were in a kind of a daze. They never heard anything like it in this world. And a lot of them say they will hardly ever again hear anything like it. It kind of put them all to sleep. And when the reel was over she sat on my knees and we were talking and talking. I suppose the *draíocht* [magic] of the little horseshoe nail worked (ibid., 112–113).

Five decades later, listeners still were charmed into "a kind of a daze" by Junior's playing. And the magic of his playing, fairy spell or no, did help to win him the hand of Cissy Walsh in marriage.

Prior to 1936, Junior would frequently play for country dances in homes. Dances were held for special occasions, such as a wedding, holiday, or an American wake—events that both celebrated and mourned the loss of a neighbor bound for America. Dances were also held when a family would encounter some misfortune, like the death of some cattle, and the charge of a few pennies' admission at the door helped them recoup their losses. The Dance Halls Act of 1935 changed all that. Jimmy Gleeson recalls:

The Dance Halls License Act came in. It was mostly run by parish priests and they made the country dance illegal. You couldn't hold them anymore. And you had a fierce gap between the old tradition of the country dance, traditional music. When the Dance Halls Act came in, it was all modern music—waltzes, quicksteps, and that kind of stuff—and there was a big lapse in the traditional music for about twenty or thirty years . . . It was a great way for the parish priests and the parish as a whole to collect money. (J. Gleeson in discussion with authors, June 2001).

To compete with the big bands performing in the church halls, traditional musicians joined into large ensembles called *céilí* bands, consisting of up to twenty players on traditional instruments like fiddle, flute, accordion, and bagpipes, augmented by piano and drum set. These bands performed for parish-sponsored dances and later, for competitions. Junior, along with his friends Willie Clancy, Josie Hayes, Paddy Galvin, and many others, played in the Laichtín Naofa Céilí Band from 1954 to 1962, winning the national Oireachtas Céilí Band competition in 1956 (Munnelly 1998, 71).

ACTIVITY 1.3   *Listen to this 1937 recording of the Dublin Metropolitan Garda Céilí Band on CD track 4 to hear the large group sound. On this selection, the group plays three hornpipes: "The Sunshine," "Humors of Castle Bernard," and "Dick Sands."*

For more informal playing in smaller ensembles, traditional musicians met in pubs like Gleesons. Admission could not be charged; players received hospitality in the form of sandwiches, soup, sausages, and drink. Junior was the central player in the ensemble, which included Josie Hayes (flute), Michael Downes (fiddle), Paddy Galvin (fiddle), Pat Kelly (*bodhrán* or frame drum), and Mike Cleary (flute). These kinds of informal pub sessions grew increasingly popular after the 1950s, with the demise of the country dances and house parties in the homes and the outdoor crossroads dances. Today, pubs are considered the major context for informal music making, and traditional music sessions are found in pubs throughout Ireland and the Irish diaspora.

Jimmy Gleeson expanded his small pub to its present size in 1978 so that it could accommodate music making, dancing, and social functions. The Sunday night sessions became a permanent fixture in the new space, attracting musicians from all over Ireland, America, and England who were always welcome to sit in. The session has continued to be a mecca for traditional musicians, singers, and dancers even as the older musicians gradually stopped playing. Junior's passing in 1998 marked the end of an era at Gleesons, but the session continues on strongly today, incorporating new musicians and hosted by the renowned accordion player, Jackie Daly.

The session documented above in 1997 is special given its place within the local history of West Clare. It demonstrates how all the strands of Irish traditional culture—music, dancing, singing, storytelling, poetry, and the art of entertaining conversation—are inextricably bound to one another in an evening's entertainment. It also reveals how music is an essential part of a community, serving as entertainment at social functions, in informal pub sessions, and as a convivial background for the negotiation of local transactions. As can be seen here at Gleesons, the community surrounding the music—including people, place, and even physical locale—is a vital component in the overall musical experience.

This session is appealing to Irish urbanites, international visitors, and expatriates who are interested in experiencing the music in its most traditional context. The beauty of the countryside, the presence of older musicians, the conviviality and interaction of musicians, dancers, singers, and listeners, and the hospitality of the Gleesons evoke nostalgia for a simpler, less commercial way of life. It seems to embody the heart of the tradition, in which individuals are highly valued within a well-defined community, and camaraderie, good humor, respect, love for the music, and love for the land exist side by side. Because of its locale and its mix of participants, this session serves as a window into the culture of Irish traditional music, both past and present: its perceived and actual base in rural Ireland, its strong link to community and history, the simultaneous presence of old and new repertory, and the incorporation of urbanities and foreigners into the tradition.

WHAT IS IRISH TRADITIONAL MUSIC?

Irish musicians use the term "traditional" to describe several categories of music and dance: songs in Irish Gaelic, songs in English, instrumental slow airs (which are usually based on song melodies), dance music, solo step dances, and group set dances. Many of these forms are shared with other European traditions, but have become distinctly Irish over time through the use of particular melodies, performance styles, and in-

FIGURE 1.6. *Some musicians, old friends and neighbors of Junior Crehan in a session at Gleesons (L to R): John Joe Tuttle (fiddle), Michael Downes (fiddle), Kitty Hayes (concertina), and Patrick Galvin (fiddle). Photo of Josie Hayes (tin whistle) on the wall.* (Photo by Peter Laban, © Peter Laban, Miltown Malbay, County Clare, Ireland)

strumentation. The major forms in the tradition were established by the early nineteenth century, but they have continued to evolve through the absorption and adaptation of new elements and instruments.

Technically, Irish traditional music is what folklorists call folk music, meaning a body of orally transmitted, usually rural-based, nonprofessional, noncommercial repertory created by and for "the folk" (i.e. not the aristocracy). "Folk" denotes music that has a long history within a specific community, often functions in rituals of all kinds, and serves as a reminder of shared cultural history and values. Because of the process of oral transmission from generation to generation, the names of original composers are often forgotten, and tunes and songs undergo a gradual process of change, becoming products of a community over time rather than of a single individual.

The American (and international) folk revival of the 1950s and 1960s blurred the meaning of "folk music," broadening its popular definition to include virtually any song accompanied by acoustic guitar. Irish musicians use the term "traditional" to distinguish the older repertory and styles from more contemporary and commercial productions. As we

FIGURE 1.7   *(L to R): The new leader of the Gleeson session, Jackie Daly (button accordion) with John Kelly (fiddle), Denis Doody (button accordion), and Tommy Mc-Carthy (concertina). Session at Gleesons to commemorate the first anniversary of Junior's death.   (Photo by Peter Laban, © Peter Laban, Miltown Malbay, County Clare, Ireland)*

will see, while the effort to define and preserve "authentic" or "pure" traditional music is an important one, the Irish tradition itself consists of evolving syntheses derived not only from Irish but also from French, English, Scottish, American, and other sources.

Defining "traditional music" is an increasingly complex task in our global economy. While it is tempting to classify traditional music as something old, passed down from generation to generation in an unchanged way, music cultures are dynamic. In the case of Ireland, traditional music and dance forms have remained distinct genres over time, but have also changed in response to both internal and external cultural influences. New repertory, styles, instruments, and contexts for performance have been created or adopted according to need, and then either absorbed into the tradition or eventually discarded.

BASIC THEMES

The complexities and ambiguities inherent in the word "tradition" fuel our discussion throughout this book as we explore meaning, continuities, and change in the world of Irish traditional music and dance. Performances today take place in a wide range of contexts, ranging from country pubs in the west of Ireland to concert halls in every major capital around the world. While most Irish musicians play nonprofessionally at sessions throughout Ireland and the Irish diaspora (Canada, the United States, England, and Australia), touring musicians and groups, such as Martin Hayes, Patrick Street, Altan, and Lúnasa, have extensive recording and performing schedules that bring them to North America several times a year, as well as to Europe and Asia. Since the mid-1990s, shows such as *Riverdance* and *Lord of the Dance* have integrated aspects of Irish traditional culture with Broadway, bringing a syncretic form of Irish music and dance to mainstream audiences all over the world.

The increasing diversity of Irish music within a global context has spawned new niches and marketing strategies in the recording industry. The term "Celtic Music" is now used to sell a wide range of Irish musics alongside traditional roots, fusion, and pop music from other areas of Celtic culture, including Scotland, Wales, Brittany, Cape Breton, Nova Scotia, Newfoundland, and the Spanish regions of Asturias and Galicia. Promoted in the "World Music" sections of record stores in Europe and North America, "Celtic Music" covers a huge range of musical styles.

But within this diversity of contexts, three themes emerge, revealing the continuities of the Irish tradition over time. The first reflects the importance of people and place as embodied in performance style and context. There is a balance between the celebration of individuality (the central regard for key individuals, especially senior musicians) and the strength and sociability of the community. This community is strongly rooted in locality, as reflected in music that praises place, ranging from the extremely local to the whole of Ireland. The music is also imbedded in the larger cultural context of *céilíing* ("visiting") and *craic* ("conversation"), in which values of hospitality, generosity, reciprocity, humor, and social intimacy take precedence over sheer musical virtuosity.

The second theme reveals the flexibility of the tradition, which throughout its history has allowed the incorporation of techniques, instruments, and styles from other parts of the world, ranging from France, England, and Scotland to America, Eastern Europe, and India. The interface between Irish traditional music and American popular music has an especially long history, beginning with minstrel shows and vaudeville, and influencing music on both sides of the Atlantic.

The third important theme is the relationship between the contemporary performance of the traditional arts and Irish history, including the long years of struggle under British colonial rule, the impact of three centuries of emigration, and the formation of modern Ireland. Traditional Irish music and dance emerged as important symbols of cultural and national identity in the struggle to create the Irish nation. Many of the contexts for Irish music established throughout the twentieth century were designed to bolster national pride in the developing Irish state. These issues will be explored in the next chapter, which focuses on Irish music from a historical perspective.

Note: Junior Crehan passed away in August, 1998, some fourteen months after the session documented in this chapter. In this present-tense account of a night of music, we write as if Junior were still alive—as he surely is, in the music and stories he passed on to several generations of musicians.

CHAPTER 2

Historical Continuities: Music, Dance, and the Making of a Nation

The harp has appeared on Irish coinage since the twelfth century, illustrating the central role of music as a symbol of Irish cultural identity. Harps were used to accompany poems and songs praising the chieftains of the Irish Gaelic aristocracy. The fact that both the harping tradition and the Gaelic chieftains died out under British rule makes the harp a particularly poignant and potent symbol of the Irish nation, and one that still appears on coins today.

The Gaelic chieftains were descendents of the Celts, who entered Ireland sometime between 500–300 BCE. Although Ireland already had an impressive civilization by 2500 BCE, most of the records of early Irish culture have been handed down from the Celts. Originally from Eastern Europe, these warriors were well established in Ireland by 100 BCE and controlled the country for over a thousand years, leaving behind a legacy of language (Irish Gaelic) and culture. Their origin legends about the high kings and chieftains who ruled independent kingdoms in the four provinces of Ulster, Leinster, Munster, and Connaught evolved into the saga literature, which was passed down orally through songs and stories.

Missionaries from Britain brought Christianity to Ireland by the fifth century. St. Patrick, the most famous of these early envoys, was first transported to Ireland as a slave in the early fifth century. After escaping his enslavers, he later returned to spread the gospel throughout the island. Over the course of the next several centuries, Irish monasteries became great centers for learning, writing, and music. Although no music manuscripts survive, it is known that there were professional schools of music in the monasteries and that the harp was the official instru-

FIGURE 2.1 *Map of Celtic Ireland, c. 800, showing independent kingdoms within the four provinces: Ulster (Ulaid), Munster, Leinster, and Connaught.* (Reprinted with permission from Oxford University Press)

ment used to accompany voices (McCarthy 1999, 31). Sacred music is thought to have developed in tandem with indigenous art music. Beautifully illuminated religious manuscripts, including The Book of Kells, were also created during this period.

When Henry II of England arrived in Ireland in 1171, beginning the long process of British conquest and colonialism on the island, music was essential to the bardic school of classical poetry. Gaelic kings and chiefs employed hereditary poets and harpers as important members of their

FIGURE 2.2   *Folio 292r, The opening words of St. John's Gospel from The Book of Kells. Notice the characteristic calligraphy and design work, including geometrical shapes, interlacing and spiral patterns, animal forms, and figure representations. This plate is often referred to as the "seated harper."*   (Reprinted with permission from The Board of Trinity College Dublin)

courts and households. Through their chanted poetry, the bards praised the exploits of their patrons, recounted their genealogies, mourned the death of warriors, and were the oral keepers of the laws. They were figures of prominence and influence, sitting next to their chieftains in political councils (Kiberd 1989, 232–235). The harpers accompanied the poems and songs of the bards and developed a solo repertoire.

COLONIALISM IN IRELAND

The early cultural history of the British in Ireland parallels that of other British colonies. As in India, for example, the British were intrigued at first with native culture, and there are records of English settlers "going native" and indigenous musicians being invited into English homes to perform. Over time, however, official views of Irish culture became increasingly less tolerant. In 1366, the infamous Statute of Kilkenney was enacted to protect against " . . . degenerate English who wore Irish costume and spoke Irish, against intermarriage and fosterage with the Irish enemies . . . " (Simms 1989, 75). The image of the Irish as "wild barbarians" became a stereotype that persisted throughout the colonial era in Ireland and in the United States through the nineteenth century.

Repressive legislation against Irish culture, and specifically poetry and music, became more comprehensive under Queen Elizabeth in the late sixteenth and early seventeenth centuries. Elizabeth felt that itinerant poets and harpers were often political spies, stirring up unrest through their lyrics. Their songs in praise of their aristocratic patrons were also thought to direct power away from the crown. By 1571, the Earl of Kildare was commissioned to punish by death all harpers, rhymers, and bards. A statute of 1603 effectively banned the playing of Irish music with a proclamation to "hang the harpers wherever found and destroy their instruments." (O'Boyle 1976, 10)

While records do not indicate any harpers put to death in this manner, the harping tradition declined as musicians faced intimidation. The increasing impact of English colonial plantations from the early seventeenth century on led to a breakdown of the Gaelic order, affecting the aristocratic harping tradition. With the collapse of the system, harpers adapted to changes in patronage by playing for the new Anglo-Irish gentry (Moloney 2000, 7). But without its function within the bardic order, the harping tradition began to seriously weaken by the mideighteenth century.

The most famous harper of this era, Turlough Carolan (1670–1738), was one of the last known players in this long lineage. Carolan, who became blind at the age of twenty-two, was a poet, harper, and composer. Pursuing one of the few careers available to the blind, he traveled by horse from patron to patron, accompanied by a servant who carried his harp. His compositions, most of which were written in honor of his patrons, show considerable influence from the Italian Baroque music of the period that he must have heard in the great houses he visited. His compositions were published during his lifetime and survive in many subsequent tune anthologies (CD track 5: "Planxty Johnson" by Turlough Carolan, performed by Sally Perreten on the harp).

FIGURE 2.3   *Carolan, The Celebrated Irish Bard. A print from the painting by Francis Binden (1698–1765).*   *(Reproduced with permission from the National Gallery of Ireland)*

Edward Bunting and Thomas Moore. In the late eighteenth century, four festivals were organized as a means to revitalize the waning harp tradition. The most famous of the four took place in Belfast in 1792, attracting ten harpers as competitors. Edward Bunting (1773–1843), who was already recognized as a successful organist and teacher in Belfast at age nineteen, was hired to notate the music performed over the course of the three-day event in order to preserve this oral repertory in written form.

Bunting was trained as a classical musician, but the Belfast Harp Festival proved to be a turning point in his life, leading to subsequent fieldwork with harpers and traditional musicians throughout Ireland between 1792 and 1809. He is reputed to be the first Irish collector to get music directly from musicians in the field, amassing a large collection of notated harp repertory, instrumental tunes, songs in Irish and English, and lore about the Gaelic harp. During his lifetime he published arrangements of approximately one quarter of this material in three volumes (ibid., 3–16).

These volumes proved to be enormously influential; they were soon recognized as the largest extant source of the old harp repertoire, documenting a disappearing tradition. Bunting's work also helped to rekindle interest in the harp as a symbol of national identity. It became a recurrent motif, along with the color green, round towers, and the shamrock, in popular songs, literature, and paintings of the time to symbolize the distinctiveness of the Irish.

The Irish poet Thomas Moore immortalized these images in his ten successive volumes of songs entitled *Irish Melodies* (1808–1832). Moore composed English lyrics to old Irish airs, many taken from the Bunting collection. While his work transformed traditional music into popular parlor music for middle and upper class audiences on both sides of the Atlantic, it also helped to set the contexts and themes for later music and poetry composed during the Home Rule movement in the late nineteenth and early twentieth centuries. Although not overtly political, many of the songs celebrated the glories of an ancient Celtic Ireland and the beauty of the Irish countryside (Wright 1996, 21–23). In his song, "The Harp That Once Through Tara's Halls," Moore used the image of the silent harp at Tara, the legendary capital of the High Kings of Ireland, to evoke nostalgia for "the pride of former days" that may not be completely vanquished:

> *The harp that once through Tara's halls*
> *The soul of music shed,*
> *Now hangs as mute on Tara's walls,*
> *As if that soul were fled.*

So sleeps the pride of former days,
So glory's thrill is o'er,
And hearts, that once beat high for praise,
Now feel that pulse no more.

No more to chiefs and ladies bright
The harp of Tara swells;
The chord alone, that breaks at night,
Its tale of ruin tells.
Thus Freedom now so seldom wakes,
The only throb she gives,
Is when some heart indignant breaks,
To show that still she lives.

ACTIVITY 2.1 *Listen to CD track 6, "The Harp That Once Through Tara's Halls" by Thomas Moore and recorded by the great twentieth century Irish tenor, John McCormack. Born in Ireland to Scottish parents, McCormack was trained in opera and made his Metropolitan Opera debut in 1910. He was famous for his diverse repertory, and beloved for his singing of Moore's songs. Notice the difference between McCormack's style and the traditional unaccompanied style of the next singer on CD track 7.*

DANCING AND DANCE MUSIC

By the beginning of the nineteenth century, references to dancing and music making in rural Ireland are plentiful. These forms of entertainment were part of the agricultural and religious calendar in rural areas of the country, and special events, such as cattle fairs, market days, hurling matches, and horse races, usually included music and dancing. Wedding festivities also featured music, dancing, and an appearance by Strawboys—an uninvited group of revelers disguised in masks and straw costumes—whose dancing, singing, and buffoonery were thought to bring good luck to the bride and groom. This old custom still lives in parts of Clare.

In addition, dancing masters traveled throughout Ireland teaching step dancing and the current popular social dances to people in cities, small towns, and rural communities. Pipers and fiddlers—usually one or two musicians at a time—accompanied the dancers with jigs, reels, and hornpipes. As the century progressed, waltzes, polkas, and sets were added to the dancing repertory. The activities of itinerant dancing masters continued in regions such as Clare and Kerry up through the young adulthood of Junior Crehan.

The rich dance tune tradition included indigenous melodies as well as airs borrowed from Scotland and England. The repertory continually expanded over time with the absorption of newly composed tunes in traditional forms. While most players learned and passed on their tune repertories through oral tradition, many of the tunes were also collected and published. Tune collections compiled in Ireland, England, Scotland, and America have preserved this legacy, and many of the tunes that date back to the early nineteenth century are still a part of the current repertories of traditional Irish musicians today. The tune repertory was also brought by emigrants to North America where many of the same tunes passed into the American fiddle tune tradition, especially in Cape Breton, Quebec, New England, and the Southern Appalachian Mountains.

MUSIC, RELIGION, AND POLITICAL STRUGGLE

The history of British rule in Ireland is irrevocably linked to the repression of the Catholic religion. The political divisions between Protestants of English descent and Irish Catholics fueled the struggle for power and control of Ireland, beginning with Henry VIII's break with the Catholic church in 1532 and his subsequent takeover of property belonging to Irish monasteries. After Henry VIII, the Catholic presence in Irish life was regulated over the next three hundred years by a series of laws that formally excluded Catholics from participation in public life, voting, and ownership of land. These laws included the Act of Settlement in 1652, in which Cromwell's army confiscated Catholic-owned land amounting to over one quarter of the country. Displaced landowners were sent to the infertile, rocky land west of the Shannon River in the province of Connaught. By the early eighteenth century, Catholics, who comprised seventy-five percent of the population, owned just fourteen percent of Irish land (Foster 1989, 137).

"The Rocks of Bawn" is a traditional ballad that the eminent Connemara singer Joe Heaney (1919–1984) associated with banishment to Connaught. The title of the song refers to a specific place, but for Heaney was symbolic of this whole rocky, western region of Ireland. Sweeney, a laborer who can't plow the fields because the land is too rocky, speaks in verse one while his wife or sweetheart seems to speak in verse two. Verse three assumes the voice of the bailiff or agent of the absentee landlord who accuses Sweeney of being lazy. In verse four we again hear from Sweeney, who feels trapped by his poverty and inability to till the rocky land. In the last verse, Sweeney ironically decides his only hope is to enlist in the army of his oppressors.

The Rocks of Bawn (CD track 7)
Come all you loyal heroes, wherever you may be
Don't hire with any master 'till you know what your work will be
For you must rise up early, from clear daylight 'till dawn;
I'm afraid you'll ne'er be able to plow the rocks of Bawn.

Oh rise up lovely Sweeney, and give your horse some hay
And give him a good feed of oats before you go away
Don't feed him on soft turnip, put him out on your green lawn;
For I'm afraid he'll ne'er be able to plow the rocks of Bawn.

FIGURE 2.4   *Joe Heaney.   (Used with permission from Northwest Folklife and Joe Heaney Collection of the University of Washington Ethnomusicology Archives)*

My curse attend you Sweeney, you have me nearly robbed:
You're sitting by the fireside with your dudeen in your gob,
You're sitting by the fireside from clear daylight 'till dawn;
But I'm afraid you'll ne'er be able to plow the rocks of Bawn.

My shoes they are well-worn now, my stockings they are thin;
My heart is always trembling, I'm afraid I might give in,
My heart is always trembling from clear daylight 'till dawn;
I'm afraid I'll ne'er be able to plow the rocks of Bawn.

I wish the Queen of England would send for me in time
And place me in some regiment, all in my youth and prime.
I would fight for Ireland's glory from clear daylight 'till dawn;
But I never will return again to plow the rocks o'Bawn.

Progressively stricter laws banning religion, language, land owner-ship, and voting rights were enacted through the eighteenth and early nineteenth centuries; the Irish responded with active resistance ranging from rhetoric to uprising. One such rebellion took place in 1796, led by Theobald Wolfe Tone (1763–98), a Protestant member of the United Re-publicans who believed that people of all creeds should join together to reduce England's power in Ireland. Tone's attempt to land French troops off Bantry Bay failed because of weather, but localized fighting took place in other parts of the country in 1798, and is commemorated in many ballads. The inspiration of the French Revolution at this time is also reflected in a large body of Irish songs.

Every act of resistance had its balladeers and poets, who served to politicize the issues, to rally popular support, and to act as historians. The ballads, which were often published on ballad sheets called broad-sides, provided social commentary on all aspects of the Irish struggle for religious and political freedom.

EMIGRATION

In order to escape religious discrimination, high rents, high taxes, and food shortages, many Irish traveled to the United States, Canada, En-gland, and Australia in search of a better life. While most of the emi-grants went voluntarily, others had no choice. The first of these in-voluntary immigrants were Catholics who were sent as indentured servants by Cromwell and his army to the West Indies to work on plantations.

The first large wave of emigration to America began in the early eighteenth century, when Presbyterians from the northern region of Ulster made the journey. Many were descendants of Scottish settlers who had been brought to Ulster in the early 1600s. In order to escape religious discrimination and the poor social conditions that affected all the Irish during this period, approximately 200,000 left for America between 1717 and 1776. Large numbers went to rural areas in the South, settling in the Appalachian Mountains.

The second wave of emigration began in the second decade of the nineteenth century. At this time, many small farmers in Ireland were turned off their lands and the widespread loss of land and livelihood crippled the Irish economy, creating a downward spiral. Small businesses closed and craftsmen, tradesmen, and artisans found themselves unemployed. High taxes also discouraged local industries, while oppressive anti-Catholic legislation and a growing population led to further economic depression. Many people decided that emigration was the only alternative.

"The Green Fields of Canada." The ballad entitled "The Green Fields of Canada" catalogues the woes that plagued Ireland at the time. According to Irish song scholar John Moulden, the song dates from around 1810–1820 and "gives a very clear idea of the forces which repelled people from Ireland, those which would make it difficult for them to make the decision and those which would make going to America attractive" (Moulden 1994, 7). Different versions of the song text locate the events in various parts of Ireland, but perhaps the most famous rendition is that of Paddy Tunney (1921–2002), the great English language singer from Fermanagh and Donegal, who learned the song from his mother, adding several verses of his own to the composition:

The Green Fields of Canada
Farewell to the groves of shillelagh and shamrock
Farewell to the girls of Ireland all round,
May their hearts be as merry as ever I would wish them
When far away on the ocean I'm bound
My mother is old and my father quite feeble
To leave their own country it grieves them full sore
Oh the tears down their cheeks in great drops they are rolling
To think they must die upon a foreign shore.

But what matter to me where my bones may be buried
If in peace and contentment I can spend my life
O the green fields of Canada they daily are blooming
There I'll find an end to my misery and strife.

Chorus:
So it's pack up your sea stores, consider no longer
Twelve dollars a week isn't very bad pay
With no taxes or tithes to devour up your wages
When you're on the green fields of Americay.

The lint dams are dry and the looms all lie broken
The coopers are gone and the winders of creels
Away o'er the ocean go journeymen tailors
And fiddlers who flaked out the old mountain reels
But I mind the time when old Ireland was flourishing
When lots of her tradesmen did work for good pay
But since our manufacturies have crossed the Atlantic
Sure now we must follow to Americay.

Farewell to the dances in homes now deserted
When tips struck the lightening in splanks from the floor
The paving and crigging of hobnails on flagstones
The tears of the old folk and shouts of encore
For the landlords and bailiffs in vile combination
Have forced us from hearthstone and homestead away
May the crowbar brigade all be doomed to damnation
When we're on the green fields of Americay.

The timber grows thick on the slopes of Columbia
With Douglas in grandeur two hundred feet tall
The salmon and sturgeon dam streamlet and river
And the high Rocky Mountains look down over all
On the prairie and plain sure the wheat waves all golden
The maple gives sugar to sweeten your tay
You won't want for corn cob way out in Saskatchwan
When you're on the green fields of Americay.

And if you grow weary of pleasure and plenty
Of fruit in the orchard and fish from the foam
There's health and good hunting 'way back in the forests
Where herds of great moose and wild buffalo roam
And it's now to conclude and finish my ditty
If ever friendless Irishman chances my way
With the best in the house I will greet him in welcome
At home on the green fields of Americay (Tunney 1991, 156–8).

In verse one, the narrator, singing in the first person, is about to em-
bark across the ocean for a better life. He looks forward to finding "peace

and contentment" in Canada, where the land is fertile and wages are high. In the second verse, he describes the reasons for his misery in Ireland: the breakdown of the economy, and the subsequent decay of community life. Cottage industries such as linen ("lint") making, weaving, barrel making, spinning, and sewing, have ceased to function, forcing the Irish to emigrate.

In the third verse, the narrator laments that landlords and bailiffs, forcing people from their homes by means of "crowbar brigades," have destroyed the intimacy and functioning of rural life where three quarters of the population lived communally in small clusters of farmhouses. The homes are deserted and fiddlers no longer play while men dance joyously in their hobnailed boots on floor and hearth. The narrator believes he has no other recourse than to say farewell to all that is now past and to make the journey with his family to "Americay."

While "The Green Fields of Canada" begins as a lament, the final verses brim with hopeful anticipation. Here the narrator catalogues the wonders of life in the new world where nature yields bounty instead of blight and hunger. There are majestic trees, streams filled with fish, wheat in the fields, maple trees yielding sugar, and a profusion of corn. He imagines that life in Canada will be filled with all the abundance, happiness, and freedom that is lacking in Ireland.

In these last stanzas, the author of the song embroiders on important themes that fueled the Irish imagination throughout the nineteenth century. These themes included the belief that America was a land of promise, freedom, endless wealth, and unbounded opportunities for those energetic enough to seek them out. These romanticized images contrasted starkly with the reality at home, where dispossession, poverty, religious intolerance, and the dominance of the landed elite were the norm.

ACTIVITY 2.2   Listen to Paddy Tunney singing this song in the traditional unaccompanied style on The Stone Fiddle. For another version, listen to Andy Irvine's rendition on Planxty's Cold Blow and the Rainy Night.

"*Edward Connors.*"   Over one million Irish emigrated to North America between 1815 and 1844. Like the narrator in the "The Green Fields of Canada," many headed to Canada, because transport to this British colony was cheaper than a direct passage to Boston or New York.

While the narrator in "The Green Fields of Canada" imagines the bounty of the natural world, most of the Irish immigrants, themselves from rural areas, ended up in cities where there was a need for unskilled, manual laborers. They also provided labor for the creation of new transportation routes—building roads, railroads, and canals.

Many immigrants found work, but others did not, as is evident from the next song, "Edward Connors" (CD track 8, sung by Andy Irvine).

Edward Connors
Come all you loyal Irishmen and listen all for a while
All you that wants to emigrate and leave the Emerald Isle
A kind advice I will give you which you must bear in mind
How you will be forsaken when you leave your land behind.

FIGURE 2.5 *Andy Irvine.* *(Used with permission by Andy Irvine. Copyright by [photo taken by]: Shigeru Suzuki)*

My name is Edward Connors and the same I'll ne'er disown
I used to live in happiness near unto Portglenone
I sold my farm as you will hear, which grieves my heart full sore
And I sailed away to Amerikay; I left the Shamrock Shore.

For my mind it was deluded by letters that were sent
By those that a few years ago to Canada had went
They said that they like princes lived and earning gold galore
And they laughed at our misfortunes here all on the Shamrock Shore.

So it's with my wife and my family to Belfast I went down
I booked our passage on a ship, to Quebec she was bound
My money it was growing short when I laid in sea store
But I thought my fortune would be won if I reached the other shore.

When we were scarce three days at sea a storm it soon arose
It threw our ship on her beam ends and woke us from our repose
Our sea store then it was destroyed by water that down did pour
How happy we would then have been all on the Shamrock Shore.

And when we were nine long days at sea our sea store was all gone
And there upon the ocean wide with nowhere for to run
But for our captain's kindliness, he kindly gave us more
We would have died with hunger 'ere we reached the other shore.

And it's when we landed in Quebec the sight that met our eyes
Three hundred of our Irish boys which did us sore surprise
With a sorrowful lamentation charity they did crave
And the little trifle we could spare to them we freely gave.

We stayed three weeks in the town of Quebec, hoping some work to find
My money it was growing short which troubled my mind
For I had friends when I had cash but none when I was poor
I never met with friendship yet like this on the Shamrock Shore.

Well we stayed around in Quebec town till our money it was all gone
Still hoping for employment, but work we could find none
And in that place it was the case with many hundreds more
Who 'oft times wished that they were home all on the Shamrock Shore.

So come all who are intending now strange countries for to roam
Bear in mind you have as good as Canada at home

Before that you cross over the main where foam and billows roar
Think on the happy days you spent all on the Shamrock Shore.

Like "The Rocks of Bawn," this song was composed in the popular nineteenth-century genre of "come all ye" ballads that give warning or impart a moral lesson. Narrated in the first person by a man who has made the crossing to America, the composer begins by warning listeners of the poor reward they will receive for leaving Ireland. His story unfolds over the next nine verses as he explains how he and his family sold their farm in northern Ireland, misled by letters from emigrants already in America. As people rarely returned from America in those days, such letters were one of the only forms of communication across the Atlantic. Many exaggerated the truth, perpetuating the myth that the streets of America were "lined with gold."

In this song, Edward Connors and his wife appear to be voluntary emigrants, with a farm to sell and the money to buy tickets for the four to six week passage to North America. But after only three days on board, they lose most of their "sea store" (provisions for the trip) during a storm. Connors describes the generosity of the captain who supplies them with food, but other passengers making similar voyages were not so lucky. During slow passages across the Atlantic, where adverse winds could prolong the trip to up to a hundred days, hunger and disease were not unusual. When the Great Famine swelled the ranks of the emigrants at mid-century, many died on what were called "coffin ships" before reaching the other shore.

The Great Famine (1845–50), also called An Gorta Mór (The Great Hunger), was originally caused by the failure of the potato crop due to a fungal blight, which was especially devastating because the potato was central to the Irish diet. The British colonial government grossly, and many scholars say purposefully, mishandled the situation, including the basic distribution of food, so that over one million people died, either directly from starvation or from diseases related to malnutrition. Approximately 1.6 million were forced to emigrate, the majority bound to North America.

The last half of the song describes the shock and surprise of arrival in Quebec. Instead of being greeted by the successful compatriots he expects, Connors meets unemployed Irishmen begging for charity. Unable to find work, he laments that as his money grows scarce, his so-called friends abandon him. In the penultimate verse, he regrets making the trip, and like so many other emigrants before him, sorrowfully wishes he were back at home.

The message of this song resonated with nineteenth century Irishmen on both sides of the Atlantic. It served as a warning to those contemplating emigration, and united emigrants who had already experienced the hardships of the exile it describes. Over time, ballads like "Edward Connors" and "The Green Fields of Canada" grew beyond personal stories; they became expressive symbols of shared experience, creating identity, and reinforcing community. When sung today by Irish and Irish-American singers, the songs keep alive this sense of shared history and common roots.

ACTIVITY 2.3   Compare the performance of "Edward Connors" with the more traditional, unaccompanied performance of "Rocks of Bawn." What are the differences in meter, timbre, texture, tempo, and overall singing style?

NATIONALISM

The Great Famine dramatically changed Irish life. Although there were no more blights, continuing poverty, evictions, and a lack of industrialization made emigration a necessity. Approximately three million more Irish came to America between 1855 and the First World War. The overall population in Ireland was reduced from 8.5 million in 1845 to less than half that in 1914. Most of those forced to leave never saw their native land or family again.

In Ireland, life had to be reconstructed after the terrible suffering of the Great Famine and massive emigration. Along with promoting education and land reform, a growing political campaign advocated Home Rule or self-government. The Irish Party, under the leadership of Charles Steward Parnell in the mid-1880s, brought many factions together for this common purpose. Although party unity disintegrated after Parnell was forced to step down in 1890, the nationalist movement was set in motion.

Ireland was not alone in promoting a nationalist agenda; the nineteenth century saw the formation of nation states throughout Europe. In the process of creating independent countries, emerging nations promoted that which was distinctive about their own cultures, including indigenous traditions such as language, religion, music, and art. Politicians, scholars, writers, and artists of the time looked away from the effects of the Industrial Revolution to focus on images of nature, the simple life, a glorious past, and the culture of the unspoiled country "folk" to inspire nationalist identity and community. Although the art of the period often idealized folk culture as a vibrant symbol of national identity, its advocates were in most cases members of the urban intellectual elite.

Home Rule and the Gaelic League. The supporters of the Home Rule movement used both the Irish language and the glories of the Gaelic past to promote their nationalist agenda. The Celtic revival was fueled by literary figures including William Butler Yeats and John Synge, who were active in the formation of the Irish National Theatre Society. The new literature affirmed the heroic traditions of the Celtic past, and mythological characters such as Cúchulainn, the hero of the eighth century *Táin Bó Cuailnge*, symbolized the potential power and heroism of the Irish in the present. In addition, archeological discoveries of ancient Celtic works of art, and the ornate calligraphy and designs found on old Celtic crosses and in the Books of Kells and Durrow, were felt to further represent the distinctiveness and genius of the Irish people. They were copied and reproduced on all kinds of design work, from jewelry to dance costumes, in an attempt to create a national style based on the great artistic achievements of the past.

One of the first organizations to promote the regeneration of the nation "by a return to its creative source" was the Gaelic League, founded in 1893 (Hutchinson 1987, 116). Its primary purpose was to promote the values of the Irish folk through a revival of the Irish language, although traditional music and dance were also viewed as important components. From the beginning, traditional music, song, step dance, and participatory dance were considered essential recreations "to sweeten the pill" of language learning (Carolan 1990) and to bring people together into a community.

After members of the League decided to revive the ancient Gaelic festivals, the Music Festival Association was founded in 1895 (McCarthy 1999, 73). Based on a Welsh model, the first *Feis Ceoil* (pronounced "fesh keol") was held in Dublin in 1897 in order "to promote the study and cultivation of Irish music" by holding competitions and offering prizes (ibid., 73–74). The *Feis Ceoil* represented all genres of Irish music, including European classical music, but it served to elevate the status of traditional music. The competitions became immensely popular and were promoted in schools as a way to actively involve children in their native cultural heritage.

R. T. White, Printer, 45 Fleet Street, Dublin.

FIGURE 2.6   *Front cover of the Syllabus for the Dublin Feis Ceoil in 1927. Notice the Celtic designs and calligraphy, as well as the harp at the top.* (Reprinted with permission from the Irish Traditional Music Archive, Dublin)

Irish step dancing also became part of the *Feis* and the first official dance competition was held in 1897. Social dance was considered an important recreation that "brought in more people than did the intellectual debates and rhetoric" (Meyer 1995, 30). While the sets were popular at the time, an effort was made to create new purely Irish dances from older Gaelic Scottish and Irish models and reject the sets as foreign imports. The new group dances were christened as *céilí* dances, and became enormously popular in Ireland and throughout the Irish diaspora.

ACTIVITY 2.4   *Learn the figures and steps of the well known céilí dance, "The Walls of Limerick" on our website: www.oup.com/us/global music.*

New organizations, publications, and competitions devoted to Irish traditional music and dance helped to remove the stigma from these traditions. The British had labeled Irish culture as "barbarian" and "primitive" for centuries, and many Irish urbanites and emigrants to America also viewed traditional music as backward and uncultured. This attitude began to change during the last decade of the nineteenth century, when traditional music emerged in both Ireland and the United States as a respected symbol of Irish identity.

Constructing an Irish Ireland.   The 1916 Easter Rising marked a turning point in the fight for a free Irish state. After approximately one thousand rebels captured strategic buildings in Dublin on Easter Monday and proclaimed Irish independence, some eighteen thousand British troops were brought in to put them down. Later, the British executed many of the rebel leaders, and it was their martyrdom that galvanized the struggle for Irish independence. After two years of a bloody Anglo-Irish war (1919–1921), independence was finally achieved, but at a price: the country was to be partitioned into two parts, north and south.

In 1922, the process was formalized with the founding of the Irish Free State, giving twenty-six of Ireland's thirty-two counties independence, although still owing allegiance to the British crown. The Free State became the fully independent Irish Republic in 1948. The remaining six counties in Northern Ireland, which had a distinct Protestant/pro-British majority, remained directly under British rule. Politics in Northern Ireland became increasingly divided on religious and cultural grounds. This situation worsened over time, leading to twenty-five years (c. 1969–1994) of sectarian violence and bloodshed, known as "the Troubles." The 1998 Peace Accord brought a period of home rule to Northern Ireland, but still today, flare ups of sectarian violence and opposition to home rule threaten the stability of the peace process. The ongoing political turmoil has spawned generation after generation of topical songwriters and kept alive the rebel song tradition.

The drive for Irish national identity and unity heightened with the formation of the Irish Free State. Many of the same markers of Irish cul-

FIGURE 2.7   *Map of contemporary Ireland, including the twenty-six counties of the Republic and the six counties of Northern Ireland.*   *(Reprinted with permission from Oxford University Press)*

ture that had been mobilized during the nationalist movement, such as language and Catholicism, continued to be driving forces in the new nation. State policy intensified the promotion of Irish as the national language by requiring its instruction in the national schools. This, in turn, affected music instruction, leading to official support of vocal music in the Irish language. Traditional dance also received governmental support with the formation of *An Coimisiún le Rincí Gaelacha* (The Irish Dancing Commission) in 1929.

New methods for the transmission of traditional music developed with recording technology and the formation of the national broadcasting station in 1926. Record companies in North America also played a large role in promoting Irish traditional dance music during the 1920s and 1930s. Recordings by three fiddlers from County Sligo—Michael Coleman, Paddy Killoran, and James Morrison—were especially pivotal, influencing musicians up to the present day. Their records helped to introduce new repertoire and playing styles to rural musicians from all over Ireland, who often had little access to new music. Not only did the recordings further legitimize traditional music, they also expanded the audience on both sides of the Atlantic (CD track 9: Michael Coleman (fiddle) playing two reels: "Dr Gilbert/The Queen of May").

Although government support for Irish traditional music increased with the formation of the Irish Folklore Commission in 1935, that year also saw passage of the infamous "Dance Halls Act" that outlawed informal house and crossroads dances. Ironically, as the Folklore Commission began collecting and recording all types of folklore, traditional music and dance declined in the countryside, repressed by the passage of the Dance Halls Act and the growing popularity of more modern musical genres. It wasn't until the 1950s and 1960s that traditional musicians began to find new contexts and support for their playing.

CONCLUSION

Governmental sponsorship, new performance contexts and styles, commodification, and influences from outside Ireland transformed the world of Irish traditional music in the twentieth century. Many developments were consciously designed to bolster national pride in the developing Irish state; others came about through the commercial success of Irish musicians on the concert stage. But while styles have changed to accommodate new contexts for performance—historical themes, images, and repertory persist. As dance tunes and songs are handed down, they transmit memories, creating an important interface between past and present. Irish musicians, both in traditional music and in popular genres, draw on a collective sense of history to revitalize and personalize experiences shared over time. Even Irish rock musicians draw on the tradition, incorporating historical themes in new songs that speak to the contemporary Irish world.

ACTIVITY 2.5 *Listen to "Thousands are Sailing" from* If I Should Fall From Grace With God *by the Pogues. WEA, 1988. Philip Chevron, a member of this punk-Irish band evokes the emigrant experience as a seamless process over time, in which contemporary Irish emigrants not only have to deal with the memories and "ghosts" of exiles past, but also have to struggle with some of the same obstacles today.*

For a contemporary topical song in the rock idiom, listen to U2's "Sunday Bloody Sunday," about the ongoing conflict in Northern Ireland, relating specifically to a civil rights march in Derry in 1972 in which fourteen people were killed. From U2 Live: Under A Blood Red Sky. *Island Records, 1983.*

Northern Irish singer/songwriter Tommy Sands is one of many musicians who write songs about peace and reconciliation in Northern Ireland. Listen to his classic "There Were Roses," from Singing of the Times *(1985) and "The Music of Healing" performed with Pete Seeger from* The Heart's A Wonder *(1995).*

CHAPTER 3

Passing on the Tradition

This chapter will explore the interface between past and present by examining the ways in which musicians pass on their tradition. Over the last hundred years, musicians have learned to sing and play in a variety of ways, including the kinds of personal and oral transmission exemplified in the life of Junior Crehan, aural transmission through the use of recordings, and the organization of more formal learning institutions. This chapter will discuss three contexts for transmission: informal learning from family members, neighbors and friends, music competitions, and music schools.

LEARNING BY OSMOSIS: MARY MACNAMARA AND KEVIN CRAWFORD

While new contexts for performance added a more formal dimension to the transmission of music in the twentieth century, the importance of people and place still permeates the whole world of Irish traditional music making—where one learns a tune and from whom, with whom one plays, and in what setting. Because most repertory is learned by ear, the process is often a highly personal and social one, in which older players are treated with affection and respect. In a tradition based on orality, elder musicians serve as important links to the past. Not only are they role models and teachers of repertory, style, and technique, but they also pass on social behavior and history. Their stories about local folklore and important musicians in previous generations convey knowledge that precedes their own time. The settings for telling these stories and playing tunes reveals another important constant in musical transmission: the value placed on music making as an informal and social activity, rather than a professional one.

Pubs are the favored contexts for music sessions today, but house parties were the setting for much music making and listening in the past. Many musicians recall that informal get-togethers in the kitchen with family and neighbors, filled with conversation, stories, songs, tunes, and food, gave them their music. Music learning in this kind of environment is a natural process of osmosis. Concertina player Mary MacNamara recalls this kind of informal context for making music in rural East Clare:

> My father would take us, when we got to the stage we could go out and play, he would go to different houses . . . maybe twice a week and we'd sit down and we'd listen to these musicians. And listen to the stories they had to tell, listen to them playing. We'd have the tea and the corncake and all the rest, and then we'd play a few tunes with them, might dance a set. And that's really how we got our music. It was kind of given to us by the older people more than having actually sat down and consciously learned it. We learned an awful lot of things from these people without realizing we were learning at that time. And actually, we picked up the style (MacNamara in discussion with authors, 2001).

Although she learned music from her father and step dance from her mother, Mary remembers these local house parties as the places she really absorbed the musical tradition. Like many other musicians, Mary

FIGURE 3.1   *Mary MacNamara in her studio, Tulla, County Clare.*   *(Photo by Dorothea Hast)*

emphasizes the intimacy of the home and the role of individuals, conversation, set dancing, stories, and tea as vital components in how she learned the music.

Mary was lucky to be surrounded by many wonderful musicians, including the legendary fiddlers, P. Joe Hayes and Paddy Canny. There were musicians on both sides of her family, and she remembers music and dance as the first things she learned in her own home. Her father played the concertina, as did his parents, and her mother's relations were all musicians. Because the concertina was more of a woman's instrument, both in East and West Clare, she also remembers learning and playing with her extended family—the older women in her community. Most women didn't perform music publicly, although some did play at house parties, including Mary's maternal great aunt, Minnie Murphy.

Mary also equates the particular style of East Clare musicians with the landscape that surrounds them. She mentions the "fierce sweep" of places such as Feakle, Kilclaran, and Loch Graney as important influences on music making:

> It's absolutely beautiful countryside and it has a nice kind of quiet wildness in it as well. It has a beauty that has not been touched . . . But if you listen to the likes of P. Joe Hayes, God rest him, Paddy Canny, people like that playing music and if you look at the land-

FIGURE 3.2   *Feakle, County Clare.*   *(Photo by Stan Scott)*

scape, you can actually relate one to the other. There's that rhythm and bounce in the music. That's just here. I think the people themselves here in East Clare, the older people in particular, when they talk to you or when they walk into a room, they have rhythm in their bodies. They're rhythmic people. When they dance, they dance in the lovely bouncy kind of way. And it's just totally different from anywhere else that I've seen people dance. They have that lovely lift. And the very same thing is in the music (ibid.).

Mary's playing today reveals her strong tie with the local regional style. She teaches over two hundred children in the area, both in the local school and in her home, in addition to performing and recording in Ireland and internationally. Although house parties are no longer the social norm in the region, Mary tries to impart the values she learned at those parties in her teaching and playing today.

Flutist Kevin Crawford's memories of learning in some ways resemble those of Mary MacNamara. But unlike Mary, Kevin only spent summers in Ireland. The son of Irish emigrants, he grew up in Birmingham, England. His early memories of learning and absorbing music occurred during long summer holidays with his parents in the tiny hamlet of Coore in West Clare, from which both his parents hailed. He attributes his love and knowledge of music to the people he heard and the atmosphere in which he heard it:

> There were so many amazing people. There was Josie Hayes, a great flute player, Michael Downes, a great fiddle player. There was another great character who used to play the *bodhrán* and sing a couple of songs, Pat Kelly. . . . And then of course you had the really strong old people, like Junior Crehan. And I just remember feeling extremely kind of lucky to have this wealth of stuff around me whenever I'd come on holidays. I didn't really realize at the time that I was absorbing all of these things. I just thought that this was an incredible way of enjoying yourself (Crawford in discussion with the authors, 2001).

Like Mary, Kevin feels that he learned how to play by a natural process of absorption. These memories of people and place cemented his understanding of what it means to play Irish music. His performing on fiddle, whistle, and flute came later, after years of listening to his elders in the informal settings of pub and home.

Although his first instrument was fiddle, he felt more comfortable playing the tin whistle. While he never took formal lessons, he re-

FIGURE 3.3 *Kevin Crawford.* *(Used with permission from Kevin Crawford)*

members his father coming home from work and whistling tunes for him to pick up by ear. During the summers, he continued to learn tunes:

> The summer holidays were always taken with meeting up with the kind of local musicians around Mullagh, Coore, and Miltown, and for me that was where you got your music each summer. And I'd go home with my head swimming with tunes and spend the rest of the year kind of breaking them down and working them out in my own little head, and come back the following summer and be proud as punch to be able to sit in and play them with those players, you know . . . I used to all the time be striving for the summer holidays to come back and to get the chance to play (ibid.).

By the time Kevin reached his teenage years, he began playing with musicians from all over Ireland who lived in England. He came into contact with a variety of styles and repertoires through these musicians, as well as through passionate listening to every available recording. He feels that he was lucky to obtain a broad picture of Irish music through this early exposure and then through subsequent professional collaborations. While his band Lúnasa tours all over the world performing an eclectic mix of traditional and new music, his experiences at intimate music sessions in West Clare, both past and present, still represent the essence of the tradition:

The chances of your playing a really nice kind of music—you've a better chance here because you're literally going out to please yourself. You're meeting up with some really good friends. The social part is huge . . . I mean, it's not just going out and playing the music, it's the *craic* between the sets of tunes, the talking, and finding out a few old stories. You know, there's an awful lot of history that's passed down about other players. It's not just the tunes that are actually passed on in sessions. It's definitely about the older musicians. It's not as if they've passed on and left nothing only their tunes. Like the stories that go round for so many years afterwards. You figure that even if you've never met those musicians, you feel that you actually did know them (ibid.).

The contemporary pub session has much in common with its predecessor, the house party. Both are social events in which the sharing of music, song, and dance are part of a larger context. Many unspoken codes of house party etiquette survive in the session, such as deferring to older players, allowing time in between tunes for conversation and storytelling, and keeping the emphasis on sharing within the group rather than performing for an audience.

ACTIVITY 3.1 *Fieldwork project: interview an Irish musician in your area about how he/she learned music. For more details, check our website: www.oup.com/us/global music.*

COMPETITIONS

Music making has long been part of the agricultural, seasonal, and religious calendar in rural areas of Ireland. Dancing was widespread at local fairs that in many cases became venues for informal solo step dance rivalry, competitions, and dancing endurance matches (Brennan 2001, 73–76).

Festival competitions were more formal, designed to both celebrate and preserve Irish music. The perceived danger of extinction of traditional music has fueled many such events, beginning with the harp festivals held in the late eighteenth century. Competition became an especially important tool for the promotion and preservation of traditional music and dance by the Gaelic League at the turn of the twentieth century. The structure and philosophy behind the early *Feis Ceoil* became a festival model that has been emulated throughout the twentieth century.

A new chapter in the history of competitions in Ireland began in the early 1950s, when traditional music was at a low ebb. The first *fleadh cheoil* (pronounced "flah keol" and defined literally as a "feast of music") competition for instrumentalists, singers, and set dancers, was held in 1952 as a way to boost the status of traditional music, instill pride in the players, give them new contexts in which to perform, and create appreciative audiences. The initial activists were most frequently urbanites of first or second generation rural origins whose vision included bringing traditional music back into the countryside. The early *fleadhanna* (plural for *fleadh*) were held in different towns and counties throughout Ireland.

The founders of the *fleadh cheoil* organized themselves into *Comhaltas Ceoltóirí Éireann* (pronounced "Koltas Koltori Eran," and abbreviated "CCÉ" or shortened to *Comhaltas*) in 1951, and since then, the organization has grown considerably. While the central administration is housed just south of Dublin, there are currently more than four hundred branches in Ireland and ten other countries, including twenty-five chapters in the United States. The goals of the organization resemble the Gaelic League's cultural and national objectives: to promote Irish traditional music and dance and the Irish language.

One of CCÉ's most important activities has been to create and administer a tiered system of competitions in music, singing and dancing at the county, regional, provincial, and All-Ireland levels. The highest level, the All-Ireland or *Fleadh Cheoil na hÉireann*, takes place on the fourth weekend in August in different Irish towns, attracting musicians from all over the world. Most of those who attend are interested in the informal sessions that spring up in every pub, public space, and on the street around the clock. It is estimated that over two hundred thousand people attend the *Fleadh Cheoil na hÉireann* each year.

The core of each *fleadh* is organized around a series of competitions. Each competition is divided into four age levels: under twelve, twelve to fifteen, fifteen to eighteen, and over eighteen (senior). There are solo competitions on the major instruments, including fiddle, two-row button accordion, flute, tin whistle, concertina, piano accordion, *uilleann* pipes, harp, mouth organ, banjo, and *bodhrán*, whistling, lilting (using vocables to sing dance tunes), and traditional singing in both Irish and

English. There are also duet, trio, and group competitions in instrumental playing, and *céilí* band and set dancing competitions. Winning the All-Ireland represents the highest achievement in the competition chain, and is extremely prestigious.

Competition has been a major force in the sponsorship of traditional Irish music during the last fifty years and its effects have been far reaching. All of CCÉ's activities, including instruction, music sessions, publications, touring musical performances, and competitions, have brought many people into the tradition as active participants. By targeting young people, CCÉ has created new contexts for music and dance performance, emulating athletic events in the belief that competition motivates children. The long-term goal is to get the young actively involved in learning, thereby keeping alive these traditional art forms. Competitions are also viewed as community builders: at the branch or regional level, they bring people of different generations together to participate in a local community event, while at the upper levels they allow performers and their families to meet and hear performers from different areas.

For people of Irish descent living outside Ireland, the *feis* and *fleadh* are important events. Traditional music and dance are viewed as symbols of Irishness in the Irish diaspora. These art forms have been maintained as visible symbols of identity in multicultural societies, such as England and the United States, especially since the 1970s. The events are meant to motivate children to learn, perform, and excel, and at the same time to bring emigrant families together to socialize. The competitions provide a tangible link to Ireland; the ultimate reward for doing well in competitions abroad is to finally get a chance to participate in one in Ireland. For American-born musicians, success in competitions, especially in Ireland, acts to validate and authenticate their playing of Irish traditional music. Many of the well known American born performers of Irish music today, including fiddlers Eileen Ivers and Liz Carroll, step dancer Michael Flatley, and instrumentalist Seamus Egan, have won "All-Irelands."

For Irish musicians living outside Ireland, the competitions also provide an important way to come together. According to Kevin Crawford, who was born in England of Irish parents, *Comhaltas* activities were one of the only ways to meet other players because there were no other Irish musicians in his local area. However, his involvement at these events was primarily musical and not competitive:

> *Comhaltas* was essential really. You had to meet up with musicians, you know, you had to go to the *Fleadh Cheoil*, the regional *Fleadh* or

the national *Fleadh*, and there you would be exposed to a lot of the younger musicians, and lots of the kind of age groups of musicians who were based in England at the time . . . I went to every single *fleadh* that was to be had in England, but it was actually a number of years before I realized that the *Fleadh Cheoil* was primarily to do with competing. I just thought it was a great way of meeting musicians and playing tunes with people from other parts of the country (Crawford in discussion with authors, 2001).

This noncompetitive dimension of the *fleadhhanna* helped to popularize pub sessions. As musicians gathered in places away from home, the context for their music making changed from house parties to pubs, and as their playing entered a more public realm, large numbers of people were introduced to live traditional music.

Kevin's experience playing for his one and only competition reveals some of the problems, complexities, and controversies surrounding the role of competitions in traditional music today. He avoided competitions for the first few years because his parents were more interested in music as a social activity. They were used to the house parties and crossroad dances that had been the primary contexts for music making in their youth. However, he finally decided to enter a regional competition because of a financial incentive: *Comhaltas* was offering to pay the winners half of their airfare to Ireland for the All-Ireland *Fleadh*:

I decided to take part in this one competition, and I was playing the tin whistle at the time. But I was just so used to going in and being around musicians, playing a few tunes, being totally at ease with it, no pressure, nothing like that. There was never this thing that you had to go out there and play a certain role and have your three tunes. There were a lot of musicians in England who won numerous *Fleadh Cheoil* who just had the three tunes. They had these three tunes that they played and they were brilliant at these tunes, but they played them from when they were eleven right up until they were eighteen, and they won all these competitions. So, I mean I had loads of tunes, but I didn't actually have three tunes that I would have used as show pieces.

Just as I was about to perform, it struck me, that I didn't really know what I was going to do. This was a totally unreal situation. Normally you'd be waiting for somebody else to start the tune and you'd join in, or if things were going well, you might have the courage to start a tune. But now, all of a sudden the focus was on me to play my three tunes, and in the middle of the tune, I just started shaking uncontrollably on the tin whistle, and I'm not a kind of shy type of guy at all, but all of a sudden, I just broke down and I could hear the tin whistle rattling off my teeth and it fell on the floor. It dropped.

I would have been old enough, I would probably be fourteen or fifteen, so it wasn't a thing that I wasn't able to play. I was able to play at a fairly good standard at that stage on the whistle, but it was a totally bizarre situation. The adjudicator never actually said to me, didn't make me feel at ease, never said to me, "You know, don't worry about it, let's start again," or anything like that. There was this incredible pressure, the whistle was on the floor, there was nobody talking; there was a silence. I didn't know whether I was to pick it up and start again. So I just sat there and then kind of walked out of the room. And that was my one and only competition (ibid.).

Kevin's story and commentary raise important issues regarding the effects of competition. The artificial context, the pressure of the performance, and the need for polished repertory presents a radical contrast to sessions at Gleesons Pub. His prior playing experiences were rooted in a tradition in which music was a relaxed part of the overall social fabric. The rigidity and rules of the competition and the lack of any human contact between contestant and judge created a severe environment that seemed antithetical to music making. On top of that, he felt unprepared for performing "showpieces." At the age of fifteen, he was a gifted tin whistle player, but had played only in informal gatherings. He knew many tunes and played them confidently and well, but had not worked up any one selection to competition standards.

Competitions change the contestant's approach and choice of tunes. According to Mary MacNamara, this change takes music away from its imaginative and creative realm, exerts a tremendous pressure on the kids competing, changes repertoire, and demands a new kind of virtuosity:

I think people here are going in now with the wrong attitude; they're going in to win. And there's also this thing—I think parents are pushing their children too hard. You know, you have people ringing you up and saying, "Well, my Johnny is playing in such and such competition, if I pay you X, Y, Z, can you give him three winning tunes? The tunes that you think might win." That's going on you know (MacNamara in discussion with authors, 2001).

Unlike Kevin, Mary competed in many *fleadhanna* while growing up and won two All-Irelands. She now teaches students who compete at all levels, but she wants her students to play for the "pure love of the music" instead of thinking about winning or losing. She also rejects the current standards for stage etiquette that demand silence and uniformity of movement during group performances:

> When I put my kids in, the students I have, I put them on stage in the most open fashion possible, just to highlight that it's the music that matters. And that when they sit down they have their little chat before they play and a little consultation with the adjucator, and that they play their music for sheer love and pleasure, true love to the audience, not knocking it out in little forms that it just comes out so smooth. And you know, music should be played to hit off the walls. It should bounce back, it should have character, it should have personality, and in turn, create that atmosphere like in a room (ibid.).

The effects of competition on the life of Irish traditional music and dance are vehemently debated today. Kevin, a successful musician with an international reputation, falls at one end of the spectrum, with those who believe that competitions have negatively impacted the tradition. Mary is critical of competitions, but because she teaches so many students who compete, she works hard to impart her own musical philosophy into her teaching and participation at local competitions. Many musicians feel that competitions served an important function in their early years by rescuing traditional music from the onslaught of popular music genres sweeping the country, but are not needed today because the music tradition is so strong. Others point out that the tradition is strong because of the involvement of young people in competition. They feel that the very survival of the music, step dance, and set dance depend on keeping children involved in a structure that has worked for fifty years.

THE WILLIE CLANCY SUMMER SCHOOL

In late June, 2001, the inhabitants of Miltown Malbay, County Clare are busily preparing for the Willie Clancy Summer School, an annual traditional music and dance week that draws thousands of people to this small town each July. Miltown Malbay is surrounded by rolling hills and open fields, and is a predominantly farming community. For one week each year, the town is completely taken over by musicians, set dancers, and music lovers. Music resounds twenty-four hours each day in pubs, homes, tents, caravans, stores, schools, the community hall, and on the street.

During the week before the school starts, shopkeepers, publicans, and homeowners whitewash their storefronts and homes, many putting out window boxes filled with flowers. The main street buzzes with activity as carpenters saw and drill, windows are cleaned, and trucks bring in extra shipments of food and drink to local pubs and restaurants. Behind the scenes, many homes in and around Miltown Malbay are turned into bed and breakfasts, in order to accommodate the onslaught of musicians and tourists from all over Ireland and abroad. In other homes, sitting rooms and kitchens are transformed into classroom space.

Once the students arrive, music is heard in every nook and cranny of the town in impromptu sessions. Students, ranging in age from six to sixty, practice under trees, in fields, in tents, and in their rooms. The main street is jammed with cars and by the evening of the first Saturday night, all the pubs are crammed with musicians and listeners. The first *céilí* (social dance event) of the week is held on Sunday evening, and classes begin at ten o'clock on Monday morning. The classes run through Friday and the final concert is on Saturday night. The last activity of the school is a special Sunday mass with the Coolea Choir, a Gaelic singing group from the Cork/Kerry border.

This year marks the twenty-ninth season for the school, which was founded in 1973. At that time, the concept of a week-long school devoted to traditional music was new. Members of CCÉ had just begun to discuss the idea the year before, exciting Willie Clancy, a well known *uilleann* piper from Miltown Malbay. Clancy would not live to see the founding of the school that bears his name. Muiris Ó Rócháin, the school's Administrative Director, remembers discussing the idea with Clancy just two months before the latter's death in January 1973. After Clancy's death, Ó Rócháin, along with prominent local musicians Martin Talty, Junior Crehan, Séan Reid, and Paddy Joe McMahon, decided to launch the school in Miltown Malbay as a way to commemorate Willie Clancy. Ó Rócháin, a teacher and collector, was influenced by the existence of summer schools of traditional music in Denmark. He remembers how organizing the school involved creating a new noncompetitive model:

We made out the first program of the school, tentatively really because it was flexible. We didn't know whether it would work or what would be the best format because it was something novel, something new. Up to that, there had been no sort of formal summer schools in Ireland . . . As you are aware, most of us say [the music is] orally

FIGURE 3:4   *Muiris Ó Róchái̇n, Miltown Malbay, County Clare.   (Photo by Stan Scott)*

transmitted within the families or within the neighbors, and you know, there had been a few isolated classes, but this was a concerted effort to form a school (Ó Róchái̇n in discussion with authors, 2001).

The school began its first year with classes in fiddle, whistle, and flute, attracting about eighty students. It split from CCÉ after the first year, and from then on, the "Willie Week" was fully independent. During the second year, the *uilleann* pipes were added and the school's format of daily morning classes, afternoon lectures, and evening concerts was established. This structure has stayed the same through the years, with the addition of afternoon and evening *céilí*, but the number of classes has increased dramatically. Ó Róchái̇n estimated that in 2000, the school enrolled fifteen hundred students with thirty-two classes in fiddle, sixteen classes each in flute, tin whistle, and *uilleann* pipes, six classes in concertina, seven classes in accordion, a traditional singing workshop, and ten set dance workshops.

The teachers brought in for the week represent a wide range of regional styles and experience. Over the years, tutors have ranged from local Clare musicians such as Junior Crehan (fiddle) and Micho Russell (tin whistle) to London emigrants such as Bobby Casey (fiddle) and

FIGURE 3.5   *Brochure from the Willie Clancy Summer School 2001 with Willie Clancy featured playing the uilleann pipes.   (Printed with permission from Muiris Ó Rócháin)*

Brendan McClinchey (fiddle). While many tutors perform internationally, others are known locally or regionally as excellent players and teachers. Students learn directly from one musician during the week, picking up tunes, ornamentation, and style by ear. However, they are able to hear the playing of many musicians at the evening concerts, each of which features one instrument.

While the formal activities are well attended, it is the informal music making around the clock that attracts musicians from all over Ireland, Europe, and America. Irish traditional music luminaries can be found playing in sessions in small pubs with nonprofessionals and students from the school. Many professional musicians take the week off to come to Miltown, not to teach, but to enjoy a vacation. Players are there for the love of the music, rather than for material gain:

> That's one thing I've even seen in accounts written of the school, particularly by Americans. They go in here and they see the likes of Sharon Shannon and Noel Hill and Martin Hayes and all these people playing their heart out, where they [listeners] have to cue up in Chicago to get in and it was much more formal than here, where you can talk to them and chat with them and all the rest. That is a big thing, the informality side of it . . . This is a culture that is to be enjoyed, to be appreciated (ibid.).

Because the pubs are small in Miltown, the intimacy and intensity makes many of these sessions magical both for players and listeners.

Some pubs have become associated with certain players over the years, creating structure within the apparent informality and spontaneity of the impromptu sessions. Ó Rócháin identifies factors that help to create these temporary communities that reform each year. One important factor is regionalism: because musicians are from the same area, they may want to play together because they share a common style. Other factors relate to the history of a pub. For example, the kitchen of Friel's Pub is where Willie Clancy himself regularly played. However, for the first-time student at the Willie Clancy Week, this kind of structure may not be apparent as he or she tries to pack in classes, lectures, concerts, sessions, and *céilís* each day. But the rituals and traditions that develop informally over time draw people back again and again to the festival.

For the musicians, finding the right pub to play in becomes the highest priority, as the week gets increasingly crowded and the pubs are packed with too many patrons and players. Musicians are often forced to find pubs outside of town, and rely on word of mouth about a good session, information often conveyed with the utmost secrecy to keep outsiders out. The goal is to find a venue suitable for music where a small group of musicians "in the know" can start a session. Ciaran Carson, in his book, *Last Night's Fun*, humorously describes the arduous process of finding the right session on the fringes of town:

> O'Looney's is one of those subjective venues where musicians evade the hoi polloi of the designated festival or fleadh town. Established by anecdote and shibboleth, they are arrived at by elaborate routines;

false trails are laid and misdirections given out . . . musicians leave false scents, like wearing L'Air du Temps instead of Brut; there is an undercover noir to everything, as everyone is shadowed . . . As the town is saturated, movement becomes difficult. It is not unusual for a rake of musicians to play, drink, eat, talk, and sleep in the same establishment for four days; and knowing when to stay put requires some art or wisdom. (Carson 1996, 138–9).

The Willie Clancy Summer School has had an enormous influence on the promotion and performance of Irish traditional music and dance since its inception. It established a model for teaching music and dance in an intensive one-week format of classes, lectures, and concerts in a noncompetitive environment that has been imitated throughout Ireland and abroad. The summer calendar in Ireland is now filled with week-long or weekend schools that follow a similar format, but with many variations: most are smaller, some are geared more for children, while others focus on a specific instrument. Many people also feel that the initiation of classes in set dancing at the 1982 Willie Clancy Summer School helped to set off a revival of the genre that is still gaining momentum today.

CHAPTER 4

The Dance Tune Tradition

Entering a pub session of Irish traditional music, you will hear lively tunes performed on a variety of instruments—fiddles, tin whistles, flutes, concertinas, banjos, and *uilleann* pipes, often accompanied by a guitar or *bodhrán*. Although no drum set hammers out a beat, the music has an inescapable drive that rocks the room. Occasionally a step dancer might stamp out a spontaneous percussion pattern on the floor or a group of set dancers might gather to move through a sequence of figures, but whether danced to or not, the music is obviously dance music. The thousands of tunes that make up this repertory are linked to dance types: reels, jigs, hornpipes, marches, polkas, and waltzes. Although the tunes are used to accompany these dances, they are also played as pure music, independent of dancing. Many have been performed for over two hundred years, although the repertory is continually expanding with the absorption of newly composed tunes.

This chapter will explore the dance tune tradition by focusing on the tunes and the instruments on which they are played.

TUNE STRUCTURE

Irish dance tunes consist of a single melodic line. Whether a tune is played by one musician or by a group, all play the same melody. The majority of tunes are in binary form, with an eight measure A section and an eight measure B section. The melodic range of the B section usually rises above that of the A section. These sections (or strains) are often repeated when played, so that the whole melody consists of thirty-two bars of music, represented as AABB. After playing the entire tune once, musicians usually repeat it a few times before switching to another that has the same form and rhythm, but a different melody. This process of making medleys of tunes expands the melodic possibilities of a single performance.

In addition to regularity of form, tunes display interior symmetry. Most strains can also be divided into two or four equal phrases with frequent repetition of motifs between them. This inherent predictability of form is the backbone of the dance tune tradition on which players embellish and create their individual variations.

It is the rhythm of dance tunes that differ so that we can tell a jig from a reel. Listen to CD track 10 played by Mary MacNamara on concertina. She plays a medley of two reels entitled "The Ash Plant" and "The Dog Among the Bushes."

ACTIVITY 4.1   *Reel Medley*
Clap along with the basic beat. Reels are in duple meter, so you should feel two beats to each measure. Clapping eight groups of two beats, you come to the end of the first A section. "The Ash Plant" is in binary form, but the sections are not repeated, so Mary continues on to the B section that also consists of eight groups of two beats. At the end of the B section, the tune is repeated from the beginning. Clapping from the beginning, count to yourself or aloud 1-2, 2-2, 3-2, 4-2, 5-2, 6-2, 7-2, 8-2 for section A, and the same for section B; keep clapping through the three times the tune is played (ABABAB).

Notice that after three times through "The Ash Plant," Mary switches without pause to the next tune, "The Dog Among the Bushes." It has the same reel rhythm, but a different melody. This tune is performed with repeated sections (AABB), each eight measures long. Listen to each change of section. Notice that the B section is higher in pitch than the A section.

TUNE COLLECTIONS

Two primary motivations—the need to preserve the repertoire and a growing sense of nationalism—led to the collecting and publishing of tune collections in Ireland, beginning with the Dublin publication of John and William Neale's *Collection of the Most Celebrated Irish Tunes* in 1724. Many other collections followed. The collectors concerned with preservation and nationalist goals wrote for a musically literate public that was, for the most part, outside the tradition (Breathnach 1986, 2).

Other collectors were musicians who assembled collections for fellow performers.

The most important tune collections for modern Irish musicians are the volumes by Francis O'Neill, an Irish immigrant who settled in Chicago in 1871. In his early life O'Neill was daring and enterprising: he traveled around the world working on boats before the age of twenty-one, was shipwrecked on an island in the mid-Pacific, herded flocks of sheep in the Sierra Nevada of California, and was a sailor on the Great Lakes. After his move to Chicago, he enlisted in the Chicago Police Force, gradually rising in the ranks to become Chief of Police in 1901. He was also an avid musician—both a flute and fiddle player—and his recruitment of musicians to the police force helped Chicago to become a center for traditional musicians from every county in Ireland (Carolan 1997, 5–12).

O'Neill began to collect tunes in the 1880s. In collaboration with fiddler James O'Neill and pianist Selena O'Neill, who did all the musical transcriptions, Francis O'Neill assembled tunes from his own memory, from the playing of other musicians, and from other printed sources. The first collection, *O'Neill's Music of Ireland*, containing 1850 dance tunes and airs, was published in 1903 by Lyon and Healy. Another collection, *The Dance Music of Ireland*, was published in 1907 as a cheaper alternative to the first volume. *The Dance Music of Ireland* had a wide circulation in America and Ireland, and is a primary source book for traditional musicians up to the present day. O'Neill's tune collections have long been a source of national pride for Irish musicians at home and abroad, and they served to raise the status of traditional music at a time when it was considered backward (ibid., 55).

Although published tune collections are an important means of preserving and disseminating tune repertory, the format of these collections contributes to the ongoing practice of learning the music by ear and passing it on by oral transmission. Most collectors present tunes as a single melodic line without indications of instrumentation, style, variation, or ornamentation. In practice, most tune collections function as references and memory aids rather than scores for performance.

TUNE AESTHETICS: VARIATION AND ORNAMENTATION

Musicians talk about the skeleton of a tune, meaning the basic notes and melodic shape that give each tune its own identity. However, in

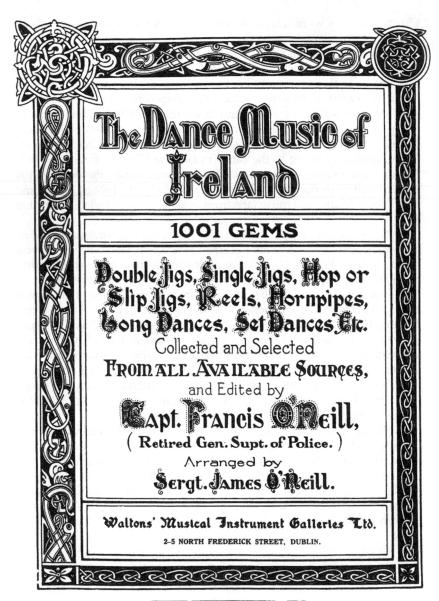

FIGURE 4.1 *Title page and first page of double jigs from O'Neill's* The Dance Music of Ireland.

FIGURE 4.1 (*continued*).

performance, players don't play skeletal versions. Instead, they embellish their playing with ornaments and small melodic or rhythmic variations that make each repetition of a tune slightly different. Musicians discuss the aesthetic of never playing a tune the same way twice, keeping its melodic identity intact, but playing subtle variations each time around.

The main way in which tunes are embellished involves the use of specific ornaments, incorporating grace notes to decorate "skeletal" notes. Irish ornaments include *cuts, rolls, triplets,* and *crans.* The cut is ubiquitous in Irish music. It involves separating two notes of the same pitch by quickly inserting a higher pitch in between them (CD track 11, Figure 4.2). Another common ornament is the roll, which exists in two variants—the short and long roll. The short roll is played within the duration of one quarter note, beginning on the note above the skeletal melody note (CD track 11, Figure 4.2). The long roll is made up of five quick notes that replace a single dotted quarter note. The main melody note is sounded three times with the addition of an upper note and a lower note inserted in between (CD track 11, Figure 4.2).

Triplets are another common ornament used by all instrumentalists. When using triplets, instrumentalists replace one note with three: either a single note played three times or three quick notes moving either upward or downward in a scale-wise progression (CD track 11, Figure 4.2). The cran is an ornament that originated with the *uilleann* pipes, but is used also on the whistle, flute, fiddle, and by some accordion and concertina players (CD track 11, Figure 4.2).

Other types of variation occur when players alter the melody by changing or adding a few notes in a given tune. Pipers, flute players, and tin whistle players often use octave transposition (playing a given note an octave higher or lower) to vary a tune in performance. They also use both finger and breath vibrato to alter the sound of a given tone. These changes are subtle so as not to alter the structure of the melody, but they reveal the creativity and individuality of the player.

TUNE NAMES AND TUNE TYPES

Tune names also give flavor to the tradition, revealing a multitude of facts about daily life, people, places, and activities. Some titles invoke a place, like the "Dublin Reel," "Glencolmcille," or the "Roscommon Reel." Another category links 'maids,' 'lasses,' 'lads,' 'boys,' or 'girls' with a place name, such as "The Galway Lasses," "London Lasses," or "Boys of the Lough." In keeping with the personal nature of Irish mu-

1. cut

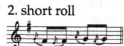

2. short roll

3. long roll

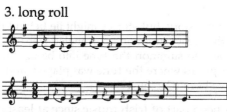

Beginning of "The Kid on the Mountain"
with long rolls and a cut.

4. triplet

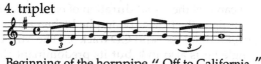

Beginning of the hornpipe " Off to California."

4. cran

FIGURE 4.2   *Common ornaments: cut, short roll, long roll, triplet, and cran.*

sic, the largest category of tune names refers to individuals, such as "Garrett Barry's Jig," "Martin Wynne's Reel," or "Pádraig O'Keefe's Slide." Often the people named are musicians who are known to have composed the tune, played it often, or inspired its composition. Still other tune names refer to Irish commonplaces or situations: "The Rainy Day," "A Cup of Tea," "My Love is in America," "Tie the Bonnet," and "The Pipe on the Hob." Other tune names are either humorous or incongruous, such as "The Hag at the Kiln," "Good Morning to Your Nightcap," and "Jenny Dang the Weaver."

Although there are thousands of tune names that conjure up a myriad of images and references, it is important to note that the names themselves do not, for the most part, describe the musical action of the tune. As Ciaran Carson so eloquently describes them, tune names are instead "tags, referents, snippets of speech which find themselves attached to musical encounters":

> . . . the tune is not a story, but stories might lie behind the tune. For, as mnemonics, the names summon up a tangled web of circumstances; they not only help to summon the tune into being, but recall other times and other places where the tune was played, and the company there might have been (Carson 1996, 7).

Jig. The jig has been part of Irish music since at least the seventeenth century. Four variants of the jig currently exist in the Irish music and dance repertory: the double jig, single jig, slip jig, and slide. All are defined by their rhythms in compound meters in which each beat consists of a subgroup of three pulses.

The double jig is in ⅜ and is characterized by two groups of three eighth notes per measure. If you say the mnemonic phrase "rashers and sausages" you can feel the equal duration of each syllable. Unless specified, the double jig is the tune type implied when a jig is called for (CD track 18: "Garret Barry's Jig" and CD track 3: "The Mist Covered Mountain"). The single jig is also in ⅜, but its predominant rhythmic pattern consists of a quarter note followed by an eighth note (CD track 12: "Road to Lisdoonvarna"). The slip jig or hop jig is in ⅜, and also has a corresponding dance form that is performed today by female dancers in soft shoes (CD track 13: "A Fig for a Kiss").

The single jig rhythmic pattern (quarter note-eighth note) is also characteristic of the slide. Slides are typically in ⅛, and performed faster than single jigs. Distinctive repertories of slides and polkas come from the Sliabh Luachra region of County Kerry (CD track 14: "O'Keefe's Slide").

Reel. Reels are the most popular tune type in the Irish traditional repertory today. The term also describes solo step and group dances using this tune type as musical accompaniment. The reel was played as the "reill" in Scotland by the late sixteenth century and brought in its modern form to Ireland by the late eighteenth century. Many of the older reels in the repertory are of Scottish origin, but Irish reels began to appear in print by the end of the eighteenth century. Tunes such as "Miss McLeod's Reel," "The Flowers of Edinburgh," and "Rakish Paddy" are examples of Scottish reels that have long been popular in Ireland. Reels are in duple time, usually written in ⁴₄ (common time), but felt in two (²₂ or cut time), with an accent on the first and third quarter notes in each measure. They are usually in binary form, with the same overall structure as the jig.

CD track 15 is a medley of reels entitled "The Reel of Rio" and "The Woman of the House" played by flutist Kevin Crawford. His description of the lineage of these tunes demonstrates the importance of people and place in the tradition:

> Oh, [they are] very, very Clare based, these. The second one was a very strong favorite of Bobby Casey, a great fiddle player from Annagh, just outside Miltown Malbay. The first tune there, "The Reel of Rio" is a tune that I would have always associated with James Kelly, a fiddle player who, although born in Dublin, his lineage would be very Clare based. His father, John Kelly, was a great fiddler and concertina player in Kilbaha (Crawford in discussion with authors, 2001).

ACTIVITY 4.2 *Clap the basic beat, feeling each of the eight measures in the A section in two. In this tune, the A and B sections are repeated (AABB). Be able to distinguish each section of eight measures.*

Kevin plays the "Reel of Rio" three times through and then "The Woman of the House" twice. Notice the smoothness of his ornaments in the long rolls in section A. Note his use of glissando (sliding from note to note) in the B section, and his utilization of breath sounds to punctuate the rhythmic flow. As you listen to the whole performance, be aware of melodic variations, especially in the second tune. Notice how he switches without break from "The Reel of Rio" to "The Woman of the House."

Hornpipe.   The hornpipe is in duple meter, like the reel, but is characterized by a somewhat slower tempo and the use of dotted rhythms. Early references to the hornpipe characterize it as a dance and a related musical form with some relation to sailors (Doherty 1999, 190). In the late eighteenth century it was probably brought from England to Ireland, where it was used by dancing masters for intricate show pieces. The heavy stepping in the hornpipe made it only acceptable for male dancers (ibid.). It was also an important step dance on the vaudeville stage in America. The hornpipe, like the reel and jig, is in binary form with thirty-two measures per tune. (CD track 4: Three hornpipes played by the Dublin Metropolitan Garda Céilí Band.)

Polka and Waltz.   The polka, a couple dance genre that developed in the early 1800s, quickly diffused throughout Europe and the colonized world. It was introduced to Ireland in the late 1800s, and became popular in the southwestern part of the country, including Cork, Kerry, Limerick, and Sliabh Luachra. The polka is in duple meter, most often ⅔, and is in binary form (CD track 16: Two Kerry polkas).

The waltz had a similar diffusion across Europe. It was enormously popular in France during the era of the French Revolution and was introduced to England by the first decade of the nineteenth century. Waltzes were taught by dancing masters in Ireland, at first in more urban and affluent households. By the 1920s, waltzes and fox trots were increasingly popular all over the island, and many dance events included a mix of these ballroom style dances with *céilí* dances. Along with traditional waltz tunes in ⅔, the melodies of many traditional and popular songs in the same meter have been employed as accompaniment for dancing (CD track 17 "Planxty Fanny Powers").

A TUNE IN PERFORMANCE:
"GARRETT BARRY'S JIG"

On CD track 18 *uilleann* piper Jerry O'Sullivan performs a double jig entitled "Garrett Barry's Jig." The first selection is what he calls a "skeletal" version of the tune—a rendition he might teach to a beginning student.

ACTIVITY 4.3   To hear the ⅜ rhythm first clap with each eighth note—the shortest duration you hear, counting "1-2-3-4-5-6." Then try clapping only on the accented first beat in each group of three, counting "1-and-a 2-and-a"; this gives you the two-beat feel of jig time.

When you count eight measures, you have gone through the A section of the tune. The A section then repeats.

FIGURE 4.3   Jerry O'Sullivan with uilleann pipes.   (Reprinted with permission from Jerry O'Sullivan. Photo taken by Ford Weisburg)

> *At **timing 0:21**, the B section begins. Keep clapping the me-
> ter. At **timing 0:31**, the B section repeats. Then the whole tune
> repeats. Try to identify each section.*
> *Now shift your listening to the melody. Each A and B sec-
> tion has two melodic phrases. Try to sense each phrase. Also lis-
> ten to repetition within the melody. What parts are identical in
> each section?*

Figure 4.4 shows two versions of "Garrett Barry's Jig," first without ornaments, as it might appear in a tune book, and then in Jerry's "skeletal" rendition (CD track 18). Although this is a simplified version of the tune, Jerry uses ornaments, especially where long notes allow time to vary both rhythm and melody. Notice that Jerry plays rolls in place of the dotted quarter notes in measures 1, 2, 5, and 6, and crans in the final measures of both sections. He also adds a cut in measure 4 of the B section after performing a roll on the pitch E. When he repeats the tune, he adds the drone pipes for variation.

On CD track 19 Jerry adds many more ornaments, including tight triplets (a piping ornament that consists of two short notes followed by a long note), glissando (gliding from note to note), and vibrato (shaking a note by rapidly fluctuating its pitch and/or volume). At the start of the tune, Jerry turns on the drone pipes to sound a sustained pitch of D throughout the piece. He plays the tune twice through, using the ornaments described. Try to notice small changes in the melody and ornamentation each time through a section. At the beginning of the second time through, Jerry also plays the keyed regulator pipes with the heel of his right hand, adding harmonic and rhythmic accompaniment.

INSTRUMENTS

The major instruments dating back to the eighteenth century include fiddles, harps, whistles, flutes, and bagpipes. Of these instruments, the *uilleann* pipes and the harp are the most distinctly Irish representatives, as the other instruments were found in similar forms in the rest of Europe. Accordions, melodeons, and concertinas were introduced to Ireland in the late nineteenth century, and have since become central to the tradition. Other instruments were adopted in the twentieth century.

FIGURE 4.4   *Garrett Barry's Jig: Two versions.*

The inclusion of traditional and recently adopted instruments in the performance of Irish traditional music reflects both its conservative nature and its contemporary dynamism. The cultivation of older instruments underscores the important relationship between contemporary performance and Irish history. The relatively recent incorporation of instruments from other traditions, such as the guitar, bouzouki, and synthe-

Second time through, with regulators

FIGURE 4.5   *Garrett Barry's Jig: Third version.*

FIGURE 4.5 (continued).

FIGURE 4.5 (continued).

sizer, also reveals an old pattern: the ability of the tradition to absorb new ideas and become more vital because of it.

Uilleann Pipes. The uilleann pipes belong to the bagpipe family—reed instruments having a reservoir of air in a bag made from the hide of an animal. The bag is inflated either by a mouthpipe or by a bellows. Other main parts of the bagpipe are the chanter and the drone pipes. The chanter is a fingered melody pipe made of wood, cane, or bone, with a single or double reed at its upper end. Many bagpipes also include drones—unfingered pipes which can sound only one note. The drones' function is to provide a continuous accompaniment to the melody played on the chanter.

The Irish uilleann pipes fall into the same family as the Scottish Highland Pipes, which were introduced in Ireland during the medieval period. But, unlike the Scottish pipes, which are a loud, breath-blown, outdoor instrument, played standing up, the uilleann pipes are a much softer, bellows-blown, indoor instrument, played sitting down. The word uilleann literally means "elbow" in Irish, and refers to the bellows which are held under the right arm and which are pumped by the elbow to produce the air supply to the bag.

The uilleann pipes are native to Ireland and developed in the middle of the eighteenth century. By the year 1800, the instrument included three drones and a regulator pipe with keys. The player, by using the heel of his or her right hand, can depress one or more keys on the regulator to sound simple chords or individual notes. By the early nineteenth century, a full set of uilleann pipes consisted of a chanter, bellows, three drones, and three regulators. At this time, the pipes replaced the harp as the "classical" instrument of Irish music, and by the 1850s, it was being played throughout the country.

The political and social repercussions of the Great Famine, along with the introduction of mass-produced melodeons and concertinas from Germany and England, helped to bring about a decline in uilleann piping throughout the late nineteenth century. The tradition was boosted by work of the Gaelic League in the early twentieth century, and again by the revival of traditional music in the 1960s. The Willie Clancy Summer School also had a significant impact on the tradition since its second year in existence when members of the important piping organization, *Na Píobairí Uilleann* (The Society of Uilleann Pipers) became active as teachers and organizers. Not only did the school provide students with some of the best piping teachers in Ireland, but it also set up a piper's workshop dealing with reed making and instrument repair. By 2000, the school attracted nearly one hundred piping students (Ó Rócháin in discussion with authors, 2001).

While the school initially provided a new context for the performance and study of the pipes, it also increased the visibility of the instrument to an international audience. This exposure was facilitated on an even greater scale in the 1970s, by the release of several albums by two new traditional Irish music "super groups" that prominently featured *uilleann* pipers: Planxty and The Bothy Band. Liam O'Flynn's playing on Planxty recordings and Paddy Keenan's playing on The Bothy Band's albums sparked a new interest in the *uilleann* pipes and Irish traditional music in general, both in Ireland and abroad. The Willie Clancy Summer School, piper's clubs, key individuals, new contexts, and new media combined to set in motion a remarkable revival of the *uilleann* pipes that continues strongly today.

Harp.   Harps have been part of Irish culture for over a thousand years. The earliest extant Irish harp dates back to the late fourteenth century and is now housed at Trinity College in Dublin. This instrument is similar in construction to those made in Ireland for eight hundred years. These harps were strung with up to forty-five brass and wire strings and made with a body of high-density wood that was often highly decorated. The instruments ranged greatly in size from small knee harps to five foot floor harps (Heymann, 1999, 170–171).

While the harp became an important symbol of Irishness by the nineteenth century, the harping tradition itself became nearly extinct. It was not until the pioneering work of Gráinne Yeats in the 1950s and 1960s and Máire Ní Chathasaigh in the 1970s that the harping tradition was revived, inspiring researchers, instrument makers, and players. Since the 1980s, Janet Harbison has been another dedicated advocate, player, and teacher of the harp, setting up summer schools and festivals throughout Ireland and creating a harp orchestra in Belfast.

The harps of today are much more lightweight than the old wire strung variety, but similar in shape and construction. Like the older instruments, they range in size from the knee-held variety to large floor-standing instruments. They are usually strung with nylon (or gut), with wire in the bass, containing an average of thirty-four strings. The body of the harp is most commonly made from cherry, walnut, or maple, while the soundboard is made from spruce. An important innovation in harp construction is the addition of levers that allow the player to play semitones (Perreton personal communication, 2002). Many players pluck the instrument using the pads of the fingers, but there has recently been a revival of interest in wire-strung harps that are plucked with the nails after the manner of the old harpers (Munnelly personal communication, 2003). Listen again to CD track 5 in order to hear the sound of the harp. In this recording, Sally Perreton plays "Planxty Johnson" (Carolan) on a harp made by David Kortier.

Fiddle and Fiddle Styles. The contemporary Irish fiddle is identical to the standard European violin. Although there is evidence of bowed instruments in Ireland since the eleventh century, the modern violin or fiddle probably came to Ireland from Scotland in the seventeenth century. With the decline of the harp and *uilleann* pipes, the fiddle became the preferred instrument for traditional music in many parts of Ireland and this preference continues to the present.

Irish fiddling styles differ considerably from one region to the next. Because Irish music is essentially melodic, ornamentation of the melody is partly what distinguishes the playing of one player from another. Each of the main regional styles—Donegal, Sligo, Clare, and Sliabh Luachra—differs considerably in how ornamentation is rendered. Donegal style is characterized by bow ornamentation and single note bowings that create a more staccato attack, while Clare style is thought to be more flowing because of the player's use of left hand ornamentation and longer bow strokes. Sliabh Luachra players tend to use distinctive ostinato rhythms in their bowing which make the music sprightly and suitable for dancing.

The Sligo style was first popularized by the classic recordings of Michael Coleman, James Morrison, and Paddy Killoran who emigrated to the United States in the 1920s. The dissemination of their bright, fast, and smooth playing style began a process of standardization that was augmented by records, radio, and competitions. While many feared the dilution of regional styles by the hegemony of the Sligo approach, there is renewed interest today in maintaining and celebrating regional differences. It is also important to remember that there are many variants within each region, and that each individual player has a personal style developed over time from all the musical influences and experiences that shape his or her life.

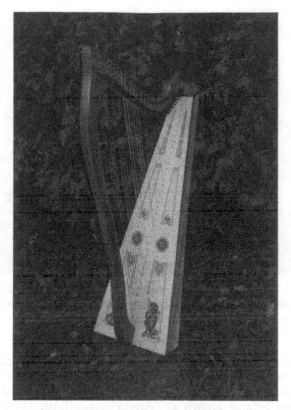

FIGURE 4:6   *Irish harp (made by David Kortier).*   *(Photo by Dorothea Hast)*

Concertina.   The concertina belongs to the free reed family of instruments, including accordions and melodeons, all of which are popular in Ireland today. The concertina is a hexagonal, button operated, bellows type "squeeze box" played with the fingers from both hands. It was developed in 1829 by Charles Wheatstone in England. Wheatstone's instruments became known as the English concertina, and were characterized by having the same note sound on both the push and the pull. Because of its similar range to the violin, it became very popular among upper class amateur music makers and much music was published for concertina ensembles.

FIGURE 4.7 *Session in Crotty's, Kilrush, County Clare. (L to R): Bernadette McCarthy (fiddle), Jacqueline McCarthy (concertina), and Brid Donohue (tin whistle). (Photo by Peter Laban, © Peter Laban, Miltown Malbay, County Clare, Ireland)*

Around the same time, a German maker developed a concertina that played different notes on the push and pull. By the 1850s, English concertina makers began working from the German model, and these new instruments became known as "Anglo" concertinas. With new mass production, cheap instruments were produced in both Germany and England.

The concertina came to Ireland by the late 1800s. Mass produced instruments were poorly made, but extremely loud and therefore good for accompanying dances. The instruments were popular all over Ireland, but were soon supplanted by the even louder accordion. However, concertinas continued to remain popular in Clare and a large number of cheap German models flooded the market there from 1900–1950. Women were able to buy them at local hardware stores, and because of this, the concertina became known as a woman's instrument. Many houses had concertinas that were used for practice and for house dances, but because of their poor quality, the instruments had to be replaced often (MacNamara in discussion with authors, 2001). Listen again to CD tracks 3 and 10 in order to hear the sound of the concertina. Kitty Hayes plays two jigs, "The Mist Covered Mountain" (Crehan) and "Tommy Whelan's" on track 3. Mary MacNamara plays two reels, "The Ash Plant" and "The Dog Among the Bushes" on track 10.

Tin Whistle. For many players, the tin whistle provides their entry into the world of Irish traditional music. Because of its cheap construction, portability, and accessibility, the tin whistle (also called pennywhistle, or *feadóg stáin* in Irish) is often a child's or beginner's first instrument. It dates back to the nineteenth century in Ireland, although whistle-type instruments date back to antiquity. The immediate precursor of the instrument was a wooden flageolet that appeared in the late eighteenth century. The earliest whistles made of tinplate found in Ireland date to c. 1825 and were made in England. Mass production was begun in England in 1843 by the Clarke Company, which manufactures whistles up to the present day (Hamilton 1999, 397).

The Clarke whistle is a narrow, long, rolled tin cone with a wooden fipple or plug. After 1950, the more common construction was that of a cylindrical brass tube with a plastic top. The best known whistles made by the Generation Company have brass or nickel finishes and come in different keys, the most common being in the key of D. Irish companies have followed this construction, but have experimented with using different materials. Irish and American instrument makers make more expensive handmade versions in a variety of woods.

Each whistle has six finger holes, similar to the chanter of the *uilleann* pipes, but pitched an octave above. Overblowing (using more air) produces a second octave. The newest addition to the family of whistles is the low whistle, which plays an octave below the standard whistle in D; it has become extremely popular as a concert instrument. Refer to CD tracks 13 and 16 to hear the tin whistle.

Flute. The reels played by Kevin Crawford on CD track 15 demonstrate the sound of the Irish flute, a wooden, transverse instrument similar to the European Baroque flute. Little is known about its history in Ireland until the eighteenth century, although it was already very popular throughout Europe. It was not commonly played in Irish traditional music until the middle of the nineteenth century when mass production in England and Germany made it more affordable.

The flute has strong associations with certain regions in Ireland. While the low number of early recordings of flute players indicates that the instrument did not have the same prestige as the fiddle and pipes, since the 1950s it has surged in popularity, with the emergence of many fine players.

Because of increased demand, flute makers began producing instruments in Ireland in the mid-1970s, most based on the old English designs from the nineteenth century. Makers today in Ireland, England, and the United States offer varieties of flutes ranging from keyless models to instruments with up to eight keys.

Plucked Instruments. The guitar, banjo, mandolin, and bouzouki are the most recent additions to the tradition, aside from electric instruments. The banjo is an interesting example of exchange between America and Ireland. The unfretted, five-string American banjo was probably introduced to Ireland by white performers in blackface minstrel shows that toured the country shortly before the Great Famine. American innovations such as the addition of frets (c. 1878) and the invention of the four-string tenor banjo (c. 1915) were quickly adopted in Ireland. James Wheeler was the first player to record Irish dance music on the banjo in a 1916 recording. Irish banjo players, employing the high-pitched, standard American tenor banjo tuning (C–G–D–A), made many recordings in the 1920s and 1930s.

The banjo was played by a relatively small number of Irish musicians until the early 1960s, when the Dubliners' Barney McKenna's virtuoso playing attracted many musicians to the tenor instrument. From this time forward, McKenna's lower banjo tuning (G–D–A–E), one octave below the fiddle, became the standard for Irish banjo players (Moloney 1999, 22–25).

The bouzouki, a Greek long necked lute, was adapted to Irish music in the 1960s by Johnny Moynihan and popularized by the playing of Andy Irvine, Donal Lunny, and Alec Finn. Although the guitar was used to accompany some of the early recording artists, including Michael Coleman, it had little place in Irish traditional music until the folk revival of the 1960s. At first it was used primarily to accompany songs, but by the early 1970s, it was used to accompany tunes. Groups like Sweeny's Men and Planxty experimented for the first time with multiple layers of plectral accompaniment, using acoustic guitar, mandolin, bouzouki, and banjo. These pioneering trends have come to dominate contemporary performance practice.

The Bodhrán.   The *bodhrán* (pronounced "bough-rawn") is a frame drum consisting of a shallow hoop of wood, covered on one side with a stretched animal skin and reinforced with cross pieces of wood, cord, or wire. It is played either with the bare fingers or with a wooden beater. One hand does the beating; the other is used either to hold the cross pieces, or to press or even slap the skin from inside the drum.

Until the mid-twentieth century, the main function for the *bodhrán* was as a skin tray for separating chaff, baking, serving food, and storing food or tools. Its use as a musical instrument in rural Ireland was restricted to ritual occasions such as seasonal mummer's plays. (Schiller 2001, 95–97 and Ó Súilleabháin 1984, 1–3). The earliest evidence for the *bodhrán's* use in nonritual Irish music is a painting of a flutist accom-

FIGURE 4.8   *(L to R) mandolin (Lyon and Healy), bouzouki (Fylde), guitar (Santa Cruz), and bodhrán with beater (Cooperman).*   (Photo by Dorothea Hast)

panied by a tambourine player from 1842, but it did not appear on the concert stage or recordings until the 1960s, when Seán Ó Riada used it in his radio ensemble Ceoltóirí Chualann. Davey Fallon, and then Peadar Mercier, popularized the *bodhrán* in concerts and recordings of the Chieftains, formed in 1963. Since then the *bodhrán* has been used by many Irish traditional musicians to accompany both dance music and songs (Cunningham 1999, 28–32). The *bodhrán* has now been accepted by CCÉ as a full-fledged traditional instrument, with annual competitions. Playing styles incorporate rhythmic devices from many sources, including Irish step-dancing, jazz and other extra-Irish traditions.

Piano, Synthesizers, and Electric Instruments. Although the piano has played an accompaniment role in the performance of Irish music since the early 1900s, its use has often been restricted to recordings, *céilí* bands, and Irish dance orchestras—commercial contexts in which harmonic accompaniment was required. Electric keyboards and guitars often fulfill this role today.

One of the first musicians to play an electric keyboard in an Irish traditional music group was Tríona Ní Dhomhnaill, who played an electric clavinet with the Bothy Band in the 1970s. Since then, Irish groups have often employed electric instruments and synthesizers. By the early 1990s the crossover group Clannad used synthesizer and drum programming on their recordings. In employing synthesizers to create a mystical mood, Clannad ushered in a wave of imitators, many of whom found a niche in the new marketing categories of "new age" or "Celtic music."

While most Irish traditional bands have consciously chosen to remain acoustic, many of the crossover or fusion bands, beginning with Moving Hearts in 1981, have added electric instruments and drum set to their lineup of acoustic instruments. Some of the better known of these Irish and Irish American bands include the Pogues, Black 47, Solas, the Eileen Ivers Band, and Gaelic Storm. Other traditional groups have experimented sparingly with the use of electric instruments, as well as other instruments from further "outside" the tradition by inviting guest artists to join them on stage or on recordings.

SOLO VERSUS ENSEMBLE PLAYING: SESSIONS, CÉILÍ BANDS, AND SMALL GROUPS

Until recent times the Irish dance tune tradition was essentially a solo or unison, unaccompanied art form. Performances by individual musicians were highly valued in social settings such as the house party. Irish instrumental music has gradually shifted over time toward a more ensemble-oriented style. As music making began to take place outside the home, the group-oriented pub session became a popular context for playing.

The practice of group playing in order to provide a louder sound for dancing began before the 1920s in Ireland, America, and England, with the first *céilí* bands and Irish dance orchestras. These ensembles ranged in size, but typically included fiddles, flutes, button accordions, and *uilleann* pipes playing the melody, and piano, bass, and snare drum as accompaniment. The Irish *céilí* bands of the 1920s and 1930s were locally based, but many were able to broadcast on the newly established Radio Éireann and to make 78 rpm recordings, as well as play for dances and other functions.

ACTIVITY 4.5 *Listen again to the recording of the Dublin Metropolitan Garda Céilí Band on CD track 6 to get a sense of the large group sound. Consisting of Dublin policemen, this band was unusual in its day because of its instrumentation, including seven fiddles, double bass, piccolo, clarinet, French horn, drums, accordion, and piano. They play three hornpipes: "The Sunshine," "Humors of Castle Bernard," and "Dick Sands."*

After the passage of the Dance Halls Act in 1935, the need for a louder sound increased as venues became larger. Touring bands formed all over the country, reaching their zenith in the 1950s and 1960s when contexts for performance and competition abounded. Performance opportunities declined in the 1970s and 1980s, but the set dance revival in the late 1980s helped to bring the *céilí* bands back. Some of the early bands are still active today.

Since the 1960s, the ensemble style has developed in new directions, giving emphasis to both the group and individual player. Musicians in smaller bands experimented with taking solos and adding accompaniment (on piano, harpsichord, guitar, bouzouki, and synthesizer) and harmonies to dance tunes and songs for their concert performances and recordings. The number of touring groups in the first decade of this century is soaring and includes Patrick Street, Boys of the Lough, Altan, Lúnasa, the Chieftains, Danu, Dervish, Flook, Eileen Ivers, Sharon Shannon, and Déanta to name just a few. The innovations of these and other musicians will be discussed in the last chapter.

CHAPTER 5

Singers, Sessions, and Songs

At nine o'clock on Friday night, June 8, 2001, the streets of Dublin are
crowded with groups of young men and women, laughing and talking
as they make their leisurely ways to their favorite local pubs. I (Stan
Scott) drive past the green expanse of Merrion Square, skirt the walls
of Trinity College, pass underneath the tracks of the commuter train,
and park beside Trinity Inn on Pearse Street. Entering the pub, I recognize the grizzled red beard of Luke Cheevers, standing at the bar and
gathering a round of drinks for some of his convivial partners in song.
Luke is a long-time member of the Góilín (pronounced "go-lean")
Singers' Club, a group of traditional singers who have been meeting to
sing on Friday nights for more than two decades. Club member Jerry
O'Reilly explains that the title góilín "comes from two things . . . an expression for singing, in Connemara, . . . and also, it's an outlet from
something out into a bigger thing. And this is what we're endeavour-
ing to do—pushing it [traditional singing] out into the mainstream of
Irish life" (O'Reilly in discussion with authors, 2001).

The choice of a Gaelic term for singing from the rugged Connemara
countryside is highly significant, because Connemara is considered the
heartland of *sean-nós* (literally "old style") singing, the bedrock of Irish
traditional song. Connemara is one of several pockets, collectively
known as the *gaeltacht*, where the Irish language has survived as an unbroken, dominant linguistic tradition. Connemara *sean-nós* singing features Gaelic lyrics, and favors highly ornamented, drawn-out modal
melodies, sung a cappella by a solo vocalist. In the Góilín Singers' Club,
sean-nós songs are heard along with English language songs, both being acknowledged as important parts of the Irish singing tradition.

The pub resounds with the energetic chatter of Dubliners beginning
their weekend. Exchanging greetings with Luke, I proceed up the stairs
to a quieter room, where the singing will begin at ten o'clock. I am
greeted by Jerry O'Reilly's wife Anne, who chats with a friend while
collecting a small admission fee from each person who enters the ses-

84

sion. Various cassette tapes and CDs are displayed on the table beside her, recordings of traditional songs produced over the years by the club.

From the entrance, one faces lengthwise down a long, rectangular room, lined with cushioned benches against the walls. Ten square tables stand just inside the benches, each surrounded by low stools. A bartender serves drinks from a bar against the short wall to the right of the entrance.

Jerry O'Reilly joins me and asks cheerfully what I'll have to drink. In the Góilín, one encounters the interplay of two sets of rituals: those of Irish pub life in general, and those of this singers' club in particular. Irish pub etiquette stresses the principles of hospitality, generosity, and reciprocity. Hospitality mandates that I be offered a drink upon arriving, generosity requires that as a visitor I not pay for that drink, and reciprocity assures that, in the course of the evening, I will return the favor in kind. The special rituals of the Góilín Singers' Club will come into play when the singing is about to begin.

I join Jerry at a table halfway down the room. A few minutes before the singing starts, Jerry moves about and has a quiet word with two singers. He then returns to our table and asks discreetly if I would be willing to sing the second song of the night. To get the evening rolling, the first three singers are prearranged. As in all traditional singing sessions, the choice of repertoire is left entirely to the individual singer, who in most cases will decide spontaneously what he or she will sing, perhaps taking a cue from the preceding song. Preselecting the first three performers gives each of them a chance to prepare, selecting a song and running through it mentally before the session actually begins. The first three songs give other singers a chance to think about what they would like to sing, and by the time three songs have gone by, the members have overcome the initial shyness that might result in a night dominated by talking rather than singing. Preselecting the first singers also gives the club some loose control over the sort of repertoire that will be sung. If the first singers have a stock of traditional songs and a grasp of Irish traditional aesthetics, the tone of the evening will be established early on, and subsequent singers will be more likely to choose "appropriate" repertoire.

As ten o'clock approaches, the room begins to fill. I count fourteen women and twenty-four men, ranging in age from near twenty to sixty-plus. On this occasion, all are Caucasian, and most are Irish; many are Dubliners, but some travel from other parts of Ireland to attend the session. They come from a variety of working backgrounds: government employees, teachers, steel workers, computer programmers, students, bus drivers, and one or two professional folklorists. The only prerequisite for attendance is a love of Irish traditional singing. Care is taken to offer encouragement to all the singers, often in the form of spontaneous responses during a song ("good man!" "good girl!" "that's the stuff!"), as well as applause at its conclusion.

Instrumental accompaniment is absent from sessions of the Góilín Singers' Club. The art of accompanying Irish singing on the harp, only recently revived after a break of almost two centuries, has not reentered common practice, and the guitar, in the minds of many traditional music enthusiasts, is associated with staged, professional (and therefore "inauthentic") performances. In clubs like the Góilín, the emphasis is on songs handed down from generations of amateur singers, whose intimate manner of unaccompanied singing places primary emphasis on details of phrasing, ornamentation, and storytelling that can easily be lost when accompaniment is provided. Melodically, many Irish tunes reveal a pitch logic that is modal rather than harmonic, and the imposition of conventional chord changes often works at cross-purposes with such melodies. Rhythmically, Irish folk songs tend to be sung in free rhythm, or with a very free treatment of any underlying meter; instrumental accompaniment tends to regularize tempo, obscuring or erasing the rhythmic nuances passed down by older generations of singers. To be sure, some Irish traditional songs are composed in strict meter with an obvious harmonic structure, and even the modal tunes in free rhythm can be tastefully accompanied with effective drones and countermelodies by musicians who have an ear for the style, but such musicians are uncommon. At the Góilín, skilled accompanists may attend and sing, but they leave their instruments at home.

A handful of core members take turns emceeing Friday night sessions; tonight's master of ceremonies is Luke Cheevers. At ten o'clock, he stands beside the display of recordings near the entrance, rings a large hand bell, and then welcomes all present to the twenty-second year of Góilín club meetings. He makes a few announcements, and the singing begins.

The first to sing is a young man named Pat, who sings a "night-visit" song in English. The theme of the night-visit genre is a clandestine meeting of two lovers; in many of these songs the young woman is summoned to her bedroom window by the tapping of her young suitor, who has braved all manner of perils (including darkness, cold, rain, and the wrath of her parents sleeping in the next room) to spend the night by her side. The tone may range from humor (the awakening of a parent and the subsequent punishment of the daughter and flight of her lover) to tragedy (the young man's vow to commit suicide because parental objections and class differences doom their love to a single night of bliss followed by a lifetime of separation). Pat has chosen one of the more serious representatives of the genre.

As the designated second singer, I follow Pat's song of ill-fated love with a humorous love song, in which a traveling man asks a young woman the way to the Blarney Stone (an object alleged to have the magical power of bestowing flattering speech on those who kiss it). The lass replies that "the only Blarney Stone I know is underneath my nose"— an invitation to kiss her. I select this song partly because it seems to fit well after Pat's night-visit song, and partly because many of the singers present will recognize it as a favorite of the late Tom Lenihan, a much-loved singer from West Clare. When such a song becomes closely associated with a singer, it is regarded almost as his personal property; others will avoid presuming to sing it in his presence. Performing it after the "proprietor" of the song has passed on can be a kind of homage to the singer, and the song takes on added meaning; singers who knew Tom Lenihan hear not only the tune and the story, but also the echo of his voice and manner. You may hear Tom Lenihan singing "The Blarney Stone" on CD track 20.

The third singer is Nick Ó Murchú, who, like many of the singers present, spent the previous weekend at the Clare Festival of Traditional Singing. Nick begins a ballad entitled "Mary and the Russian Sailor," but after three traditional verses the song mutates into a farcical contemporary account of a tennis accident. At the Clare Festival the previous Sunday, a singer named Mick Fowler (who is known for singing "Mary and the Russian Sailor" at Góilín sessions) ruptured his Achilles' tendon playing doubles with singer Johnny Moynihan and Dora Hast, one of the authors of this book. It is a mark of the vitality of the singing tradition that a ballad about this event has already been composed and performed, less than a week after the incident, but this is only the *first* account of the game to appear in song; within a week, another will be sent to the email of Irish folklorist Tom Munnelly.

The creation of such ballads illustrates the community-oriented nature of song making in the Irish tradition. Although Irish singing enthusiasts are spread throughout Ireland and beyond, the number of singers is small, constituting a mobile affinity group drawn together in various locations by a common love of singing. In previous generations, ballads about local events would be composed for an audience of perhaps a hundred neighbors who had personally known the characters in the story. The airplane, automobile, and computer have now made it

FIGURE 5.1   *Tom Lenihan in front of his house in Miltown Malbay.*   *(Photo by Stan Scott)*

possible for such "local" ballads to reach a similarly small audience of friends and acquaintances, but spread across an international landscape.

The spirit of this community becomes audible when singers join in on the chorus of a song. You can get a sense of this by listening to CD track 21, in which Jerry O'Reilly sings "The Carmagnole," a song dating from the 1798 Irish uprising against British rule. *Carmagnole* is the name of a tune and dance that were popular in France at the time of the French revolution. Irish nationalists of the time looked to France, which had declared war on England and Holland, as an ally in securing Irish liberty.

FIGURE 5.2 *Jerry O'Reilly.* *(Photo by Stan Scott)*

Some of the following lyrics require explanation: *Gallia* is France, the *tocsin* is a warning bell or alarm signal, the *Carmagnole* represents the spirit of the French revolution, and the "Great Batavian Line," was the government formed by French revolutionaries in Holland (Moylan 2000, 16). *Fleur de lis* was the coat of arms of the prerevolution French monarchy. The song describes a sea battle between the French and the English.

> 'Twas in the year of Ninety-three,
> The French did plant an olive tree
> A symbol of great Liberty,
> And the patriots danced all around it;
> The tools of murder, near and far,
> The sons of Freedom thought to fear—
> But Gallia taught new modes of war—
> And the tocsin it was sounded.

Chorus:

For was not I oft' telling thee,
The French could fight right heartily
And the Carmagnole would make you free,
Ah but you would never mind me.

In Ninety-four a new campaign
The tools of darkness did maintain—
Gallia's sons did form and train,
Which left their foes astounded.
They gave to Flanders Liberty;
And dealt their shot so far and free,
Tha Dutch and Austrians home did flee,
Which left the Dukes confounded.

(Chorus)

On June the first two ships at sea,
Did drub each other heartily,
Both sides claimed the victory
And gloried in the slaughter.
Jean Bon St. André was the boy,
The hero of the French convoy—
John Bull rang out his bells in joy,
Which gave the French much laughter.

(Chorus)

Behold the great Batavian line,
Emancipate with France combine—
May laurels green all on them shine,
And may their sons long wear them—
May every tyrant quake in dread,
And tremble for his dreary head—
May fleur de lis in dust be laid
And men no longer wear it.

(Chorus)

For old church and state, in a close embrace,
Are the burdens of the human race,
When people tell you to your face,
That long you will repent it;

For kings on thrones, and preaching drones,
Are the cause of all our heavy groans,
Down from your pulpits, down from your thrones,
You will tumble unlamented.

(Chorus)

(Moylan 2000, 16)

Jerry O'Reilly concludes this performance by singing the original French lyric and tune of "The Carmagnole." (Another performance of "The Carmagnole" is available on Jerry O'Reilly's CD *Down From Your Pulpits, Down From Your Thrones*, Craft Recordings CRCDO4.)

Although Jerry O'Reilly took this song from the recently published book *The Age of Revolution in the Irish Song Tradition* (Moylan 2000, 16), Jerry's rendition reveals the process of oral transmission at work in more than a dozen changes to the words from the published version. For example:

Published version:	*O'Reilly version:*
And patriots danced around it	*And the patriots danced all around it*
And the Carmagnole would	*And the Carmagnole would*
make you flee	*make you free*
And soon their foes confounded	*Which left their foes astounded*
Down from your pulpits and	*Down from your pulpits, down*
your thrones	*from your thrones*

Some of these changes ("And the patriots danced all around it," and "Down from your pulpits, down from your thrones") add rhythmic energy, enhancing both momentum and meaning. Some ("flee" to "free") significantly alter the significance of a line, while others ("confounded" to "astounded") create only a minor change in meaning, but illustrate the traditional singer's liberty to play with a text, as long as the central message is undistorted.

ACTIVITY 5.1 Sing "The Carmagnole" with class members taking turns singing individual verses and all joining on the chorus.

"The Carmagnole" is not sung tonight, but is included in this chapter to represent sing-alongs heard at the Góilín. A young woman follows Nick Ó Murchú's song of the singer's tennis accident with a serious contemporary ballad by Scottish songwriter Dick Gaughan. The inclusion of modern compositions is not unusual. Irish traditional singing is not static; new songs are often heard, and a few eventually become staples of the repertoire.

The next two songs relate to seasonal rituals: "Dancing at Whitsun," and "The Boys of Barr na Sráide." Irish Gaelic singing makes its first appearance in the following selection, a macaronic composition. Macaronic songs are linguistic hybrids, in which verses alternate between English and Irish. Many Irish songs in this ancient verse form were composed in the nineteenth century, when much of Gaelic-speaking Ireland became bilingual. (Ó Muirithe 1999, 356).

The macaronic song is succeeded not by singing, but by a recitation; Luke Cheevers presents a humorous poem by Percy French entitled "Queen Victoria's After-Dinner Speech." Luke's performance is lent further hilarity by a heckler, who punctuates his recitation with critical comments and corrections. The session is not limited to singing, but welcomes poetry and storytelling, and even good-natured heckling is included among the verbal arts represented.

Luke's recitation is followed by the macaronic *Siúil a rúin* ("Walk, my love"), which had great currency in the United States during the anti-Vietnam war movement under the English title "Johnny Has Gone for a Soldier." The first half of the evening then concludes with a delicate, florid *sean-nós* sung entirely in Gaelic.

After this song, Luke Cheevers rings the bell a second time, and announces that the newly published *The Age of Revolution in the Irish Song Tradition 1776 to 1815*, is available for sale. The editor of the book, Terry Moylan, sits beside Jerry O'Reilly. The bell marks the midpoint of the session and a break in the singing; silence gives way to the animated roar of conversation, and singers gather at the bar to order rounds of drinks.

During the intermission, I observe a number of posters on the walls advertising song-related events: concerts, festivals, and publications. Jerry O'Reilly makes his rounds, enlisting three singers to begin the second half of the session. When people have had a chance to talk for a few minutes and replenish their drinks, Luke Cheevers reads a number of announcements. The lights dim, the bell rings, and the singing resumes.

The singers become more adventurous in the second half. Two *sean-nós* songs follow the ringing of the bell. Terry Moylan then sings "I'm Done with Bonaparte," an intriguing selection. As the editor of *The Age of Revolution in the Irish Song Tradition,* Terry has collected and published a large number of pro-Bonaparte songs, all reflecting the hope of late eighteenth century Irishmen that Napoleon would come to liberate Ireland from British rule. "I'm Done with Bonaparte" breaks from this tradition by expressing disappointment in the French republican-turned-dictator, who never did come to liberate the Irish. In poetic and melodic style (though not in meaning), the song seems to fit well with others of the era, and I am quite surprised when Terry informs me that it was written by rock composer Mark Knopfler in 1998, the bicentennial anniversary of Ireland's aborted 1798 rebellion.

Terry's singing is succeeded by a *sean-nós*, and then by the English language song "Wondrous Mayo," representing a very common Irish song genre: odes in praise of the Irish landscape. Emigrants bound for the United States during the nineteenth and early twentieth centuries wrote many such songs. They give us a good look at the thoughts and emotions of Irishmen who were forced by financial circumstances to leave beloved friends, relatives, and places for an uncertain future in the New World. Clichés like the "shamrock shore" abound, and it is easy to criticize many of the emigrant songs for maudlin sentimentality. However, to truly appreciate this repertoire one must understand it *locally*, as the product, not of professional lyricists, but of actual farmers and fishermen who made the difficult sea voyage from Ireland to America, leaving behind parents, neighbors, sweethearts, and a landscape that they most likely would never see again.

Even among aficionados of Irish traditional singing, the discipline of sticking to "authentic" repertoire wears thin over the course of three hours. In the penultimate song of the night, this stylistic "dam" begins to burst, with the rendering of an American chain gang song. Irish singers are quite aware of the historical and stylistic connections between Irish and American folk music, and American songs often find their way into Irish traditional sessions. Singers enthusiastically join the choruses of "Breakin' Rocks All Day on a Chain Gang," and this communal spirit continues into group singing of the Gaelic choruses of the last "official" song in the session: "I Spent a Year Down in Kilrush."

The stylistic barrier collapses entirely as soon as the official singing is over. While singers talk, finish their drinks, stand, and prepare to leave, a gentleman who had earlier sung a lively, somewhat risqué Gaelic song entertains a small group of listeners by singing "I Left My Heart in San Francisco," with a strong American accent and the stage mannerisms of a Las Vegas nightclub entertainer.

THE GÓILÍN SINGERS' CLUB AND THE FOLK REVIVAL

On the day after the session described above, we met Jerry O'Reilly at Hughes' pub in Dublin. Sitting in a quiet corner, Jerry outlined the history of the club:

> The two founding members of the Góilín Singers' Club were Tim Dennehy and Donal de Barra . . . The first place that the Góilín took place, was in the Pembroke Lounge in Pembroke Street, in 1979. I came along about a year after the founding of it . . .
>
> What happened then was that around 1984, Tim Dennehy, who was sort of the driving force, moved away to live in Clare, and at that point we were sort of—I won't say we were rudderless—but for about a year or so, we just seemed to be drifting along, and the whole stage, we were at a very low ebb. The club—eight of us sat inside—and I remember somebody saying to me, "There's only the eight of us; it's hardly worthwhile going upstairs to sing." And I said, "Quite the opposite; it's more important than ever that we go up and sing."
>
> I went to Clare in July, and I spoke to Tim Dennehy, and Tim and I had a drink and we discussed the whole thing, and he said, "How's the club goin?" So [I said] "It's at a very low ebb, Tim; it's on its last legs." And I said, "I'm reluctant to get involved," because I wasn't involved; I was just an attendee at that stage. And Tim said, "Do you think it's worthwhile?" And [I said], "I think it's very important." He says, "If you think it's important you should get involved."
>
> So on the basis of that, when I came back from Clare, I contacted Luke, and some of the other main movers, and set up a meeting. And at that meeting we actually set up the structure we have now. Which is that we have an ad hoc committee, not elected. The people on the committee are chosen, people we know. Somebody said to me, "How do you get onto the committee?" And I said "You don't." You're asked; if you're the right person, you will be asked . . .
>
> Anyway, we had a meeting, and at that thing we hammered out a structure that we would have a guest every third week, and every third guest would be a guest Irish language singer. And then we would also try and produce various CDs, tapes, and things to do with singing and songs. And we have adhered to that policy ever since. And thank God, it seems the club is prospering ever since (O'Reilly in discussion with authors, 2001).

Jerry O'Reilly's account reveals important features of the philosophy underlying the Góilín. The club was created by singers for the purpose of singing. It is not a case of a pub hiring musicians to provide entertainment for the pub's patrons, but of singers seeking out a pub willing to let them use a room to entertain themselves. The Góilín started small, and only survived because some key individuals believed in the importance of continuing to sing traditional songs, even when only a handful of singers seemed interested. The Góilín's organizational calendar, nightly rituals, and ad hoc committee were created in response to the club's near extinction.

Committee membership, like the structure of each session, reveals an interesting blend of formal and informal, and illustrates the interaction of two important principles that seem to operate in every folk music revival: inclusiveness and exclusiveness. Informality and inclusiveness—the welcoming of any and all singers, the opportunity for anyone to sing, and the lack of amplification equipment, a formal stage, or a pre-fixed concert program—incorporate traditional values and impart to each session the atmosphere of an informal get-together. Formality and exclusiveness—the ringing of the bell, the function of the emcee, the preselection of the first three singers in each half of the evening, and the restriction of committee membership to the "right people," as defined by the committee—provide a certain measure of artistic, social, and temporal control.

Why do the members of the Góilín Singers' Club feel the need for a formal, weekly meeting to sing traditional songs? The answer has to do with the nature of folk music revivals, and with the particular situation of Irish traditional singing in contemporary Dublin. Ireland is one of scores of countries in which the rediscovery and promotion of indigenous music has played a key role in the creation of a postcolonial culture. The performing arts of subject peoples often suffer from a lack of prestige and patronage; a sort of cultural "inferiority complex" beset many of the subjects of European colonization, from the far East to the New World, and certainly affected the life of Irish music under British rule. In Ireland as elsewhere, the birth of nationalism coincided with the kindling of a passionate interest in cultural features, such as language and music, which distinguished the host people from their foreign rulers. Alongside of this nationalistic motive, we may place another: the desire to document waning folk traditions before they entirely disappear, and, when possible, to stimulate their resurgence.

In Ireland's case, this resurgence faced significant challenges on multiple fronts. Gaelic song and the Irish language had died out across most of the country by the time the Gaelic League initiated its Celtic revival in the 1890s. Even after independence was achieved in 1922, traditional music in Ireland fought an uphill battle, against both the continuing legacy of the colonial psychology (regarding indigenous art as being inherently "inferior" or "backward") and competition from a new source: the international spread of American popular music. In each postindependence generation of Irish musicians, individuals have had to choose between the urban, upbeat, high-volume allure of swing, rock and roll, country and western, heavy metal, or rap and the more rural, frequently slower-paced, quieter, intimate appeal of Irish traditional music. Some musicians chose one direction, and some the other. Increasingly, however, they have taken to blending the two, mixing styles and instruments from folk and contemporary sources to create new hybrid forms.

In singers' clubs like the Góilín, traditional music lovers create a protected space in which folk music is passed on in what they regard as authentic, unadulterated forms. The goal is not only to protect the music, but to perpetuate the cultural values surrounding it: social inclusiveness, respect and a welcome for each singer, a grasp of traditional aesthetics, an emphasis on the local (in songs about particular events, people, and places), and an emphasis on song as a medium for conveying history and an Irish understanding of it. To these values must be added another: the infusion of new life by the addition of newly composed songs in traditional styles.

The model for these clubs seems to come from England, and particularly from London's "The Singers' Club," founded in the 1950s by playwright, songwriter, and traditional singer Ewan MacColl in collaboration with folklorists and musicians such as Alan Lomax, Séamus Ennis, and Peggy Seeger. The motives for creating such clubs were several: to promote folk music as an emblem of cultural, national, or class identity, and to provide a forum for traditions that were in danger of being squeezed out of existence by the homogenizing force of the mass media.

In addition to competing with more popular forms of modern entertainment, traditional Irish singing faces additional competition from its close kin and frequent allies: traditional instrumental music and dancing. Since the 1960s, pub sessions featuring impromptu gatherings of instrumentalists have steadily increased in popularity, as more and more players and listeners have found inspiration in the recordings and performances of professional groups like the Chieftains, Planxty, The Bothy Band, and Altan. Unaccompanied solo singing, especially in the Irish language (which is unintelligible to many modern Irish listeners, in spite of their required study of it in the national schools), is not al-

ways welcome in contemporary pub sessions. Singers start a club to create a refuge, not only from pop music generated by an electric band,
juke box, radio or television, but also from instrumental sessions in
which singing is effectively excluded.

Singers' clubs are not the only place where traditional singing is
heard. The ancient Irish tradition of gathering to enjoy all kinds of homemade entertainment, including singing, storytelling, instrumental music and dancing, lives on in informal gatherings in particular homes and
pubs, but they can be difficult to find. The parameters of Góilín club
meetings—Fridays from ten o'clock until one o'clock in the morning,
with no instruments allowed and the mix carefully spiked with singers
who will stick to "authentic" repertoire—is, no doubt, artificial, but it
provides Dublin's traditional singing enthusiasts with a reliable source
of opportunities to hear and be heard, and a way of meeting other
singers, in whose company more spontaneous, informal sessions can
and do occur.

In Chapter 6 we will take a closer look at the Gaelic and English
singing traditions in the experience of two singer-collectors: Pádraigín
Ní Uallacháin and Len Graham.

The *Sean-nós* in the New Ireland: Irish Singing Traditions

In a broad sense the term *sean-nós*, meaning "old style," refers to Irish traditional singing in Gaelic and English as well as a style of step dancing. In common use, *sean-nós* is used to distinguish traditional Gaelic singing from its English language counterpart. In this book we usually use it to refer to Gaelic singing, but sometimes to describe the old style of singing in both languages.

Although Gaelic speech and song had died across much of Ireland by the turn of the twentieth century, the tradition is unbroken for native speakers and singers in several areas, especially in the Connemara *gaeltacht*. This being the case, the term "old style" may be somewhat misleading; Liam Mac Con Iomaire writes, "as the line of singing has never been broken the style is as modern as it is old" (Mac Con Iomaire 1999, 336).

THE LYRICS OF *SEAN-NÓS*

When professional bards sang the praises of an Irish-speaking aristocracy, the ancestors of modern *sean-nós* songs were fashioned by full-time poets and musicians, and would be more properly described as "art" songs than folk songs. Most of the *sean-nós* repertoire sung today is anonymous, probably composed between 1600 and 1850, and was maintained by amateur singers in rural areas after the extinction of the bardic profession, but modern composers continue to add new songs to the tradition (Vallely 1999, 339).

Several dominant poetic genres of *sean-nós* were adopted into the Irish language from Anglo-Norman culture between 1200 and 1600 CE. Irish secular song, like that of England and continental Europe, followed the example of the French chanson de amour courtois ("song of courtly love"), with its subgenres of the "pastoral love song," the "song of the deserted young girl," and the "song of the unfaithful wife." These themes moved directly from French into Irish, sometimes in line-by-line adaptations (ibid., 341).

While the Norman influence was strong, not all *sean-nós* lyrics originate from French models. Some Irish language genres, including laments and seasonal songs, appear to predate the Anglo-Norman tradition. The genres of *sean-nós* are several: love songs, lullabies, *aislingí* (vision poems), laments, drinking songs, humorous songs, bawdy lyrics, hymns, work songs, and topical songs. Lyrics frequently have an extremely local reference; the songs were composed for an audience of neighbors and family who had a personal connection with the persons, places, and events described. The songs do not render the facts in a journalistic fashion, for two reasons. First, the audience already knew the basic story. Second, singing was part of a larger tradition of verbal arts including storytelling and poetry, and singers were in the habit of introducing each song with a spoken preface explaining "the reason for the song" (O'Boyle 1976, 13–14).

Two important features of Gaelic poetry have had a profound effect on the form of *sean-nós* singing: the length of the poetic line, and the prevalence of assonance and internal rhyming. The lines of Irish poetry tend to be longer than those of English, with the result that sung melodies have more beats and accents per line than those of English song. Not only are the lines longer; Gaelic song sprang from a rural environment where entertainment was either homemade or nonexistent (and yet it seems to have been plentiful!). There was time to fill, so the songs themselves became lengthy, with many verses.

Internal rhyming, an essential element of Irish poetry, has found its way into many English songs in Ireland, often with comic effect, as in the clever drinking song "Paddy's Panacea" sung by the late Tom Lenihan:

> Let your quacks in news<u>papers</u> be cutting their <u>capers</u> 'bout curing the
> <u>vapors</u>, the scratch or the gout,
> With their <u>powders</u> and <u>potions</u>, their salves and their <u>lotions</u>, ochón, in
> their <u>notions</u> they're mighty put-out.
> Would you know the true <u>physic</u> to bother <u>pathetic</u> and drive to the devil
> cramp, colic, and spleen?
> You will find it I <u>think</u> if you take a big <u>drink</u> with your mouth to the
> <u>brink</u> of a glass of whiskey (Lenihan, personal communication, 1985).

Note the internal rhymes within each line, "papers," "capers," and "vapors," in line one, and the use of assonance or vowel rhyming in line two: "p<u>o</u>wders," "p<u>o</u>tions," "l<u>o</u>tions," "<u>ochón</u>," "n<u>o</u>tions," and "put-<u>out</u>." Also note the length of the lines, with eight accented syllables apiece. "Paddy's Panacea" is not a translation of an Irish lyric into English, but its English is extremely Irish in its use of poetic devices common in Gaelic poetry.

THE SOUND OF *SEAN-NÓS*

Sean-nós is a solo, unaccompanied genre. Musicians since the 1960s have experimented with adding accompaniment and vocal harmony to Gaelic songs, but by definition, such innovations are outside the "old style." Irish Gaelic differs from region to region, as does the singing, and in each region individual singers have personal styles unique to themselves. Unaccompanied solo singing lends itself to a free treatment of rhythm, since there is no need to coordinate with other singers or musicians, and this has given rise to slow, long melodic lines with a great deal of melodic ornamentation—but the *sean-nós* repertoire also includes fast songs in strict meter, with a syllabic (one note per syllable) rather than melismatic (multiple notes per syllable) treatment of text. Vocal timbre, as in the case of the late, trend setting Connemara singer Joe Heaney, can be quite nasal, but it ranges through a full spectrum including even pure, open tones that would be appropriate in Italian opera.

Listen to the style and timbre of Joe Heaney's singing on CD track 22, "The Lament of the Three Mary's." Celtic and Christian themes merge in the lyrics which apply the pre-Christian Irish practice of "keening" (lamenting) with the story of the Passion.

ACTIVITY 6.1 *Consult our website for the lyrics and English translation of this song: www.oup.com/us/globalmusic.*

"Úirchill a'Chreagáin"/"Creggan Graveyard" (CD track 23) demonstrates the sound of *sean-nós* through an *aisling* ("ash-ling") or vision poem sung by Pádraigín Ní Uallacháin ("paw-dra-geen nee oo-la-hawn"). In medieval *aislingí*, the narrator-poet described a dream-meeting with a fairy woman of supernatural beauty. In eighteenth century *aislingí,* the story was modified to become a political allegory. The narrator met a woman of extraordinary beauty in the countryside. In a series of questions and answers, she was revealed to be the personification of Ireland, awaiting deliverance from foreign rule (Shields 1993, 74, Henigan 1999, 7).

"Creggan Graveyard" belongs to the allegorical *aisling* tradition. It was composed by South Armagh poet Art McCooey (d. 1773). In this recording, from Pádraigín Ní Uallacháin's CD *An Dara Craiceann/ Beneath The Surface,* Pádraigín has sung a shortened version of four verses (a full version is available in her recent publication, *A Hidden Ulster*). The Irish text of verse one and translations of all four verses are given below:

Line A: *Ag Úirchill a'Chreagáin sea chodail mé aréir faoi bhrón*
  By Creggan Graveyard I slept last night in sorrow
Line B: *'S le héirí na maidne tháinig ainnir fá mo dhéin le póig*
  At daybreak I was kissed by a young woman
Line C: *Bhí gríosghrua ghartha aici agus loinnir ina céibh mar ór*
  With flaming cheeks and a golden lustre in her hair
Line D: *'S gurbh é íocshláinte an domhain bheith ag amharc ar an ríoghain óir*
  One look of her would cure all the world's ills.

My kind young man do not sleep in sorrow
But rise swiftly and come along the road with me
To the land of honey where the foreigner has no hold
Where you will find happiness enticing me with sweet music.

It is my great pain that we lost the Gaels of Tyrone
And the heirs of the Fews now nearby in silent tombs
Niall Frasach's good people who never rejected music
But at Christmas would clothe the poets who served them well.

My own my dear if you are fated to be my love
Promise me before we go along the road
That if I should die in Shannon, the Isle of Man or in great Egypt
Bury me then in the fresh clay of Creggan Graveyard

Translated by P. Ní Uallacháin

The "heirs of the Fews" mentioned in verse three are the O'Neills, the Armagh branch of the chieftains of Ulster. The poet sings longingly,

FIGURE 6.1   *Cover art of* An Dara Craiceann/Beneath the Surface.   *(Painting by Frances Lambe, Dún Dealgan. Permission given by Len Graham and Pádraigín Ní Uallacháin.)*

not only of bygone days under Irish leaders, but of the generous patronage poets enjoyed before British rule extinguished the livelihoods of the bards and their patrons.

Listening to Pádraigín's performance, you will notice that the texture is sparse: one unaccompanied voice. The timbre is warm and intimate, and the pitch and volume are slightly higher than that of a speaking voice—elevated enough to create the sense that something more passionate than normal conversation is going on, but not at the frequency and dynamic level of an operatic aria or a shouted blues.

Perhaps the most remarkable aspect of this performance, when compared with more familiar kinds of singing, is the use of rhythm to emphasize the meaning and emotion of the text. Just as the timbre, pitch, and volume of her singing are closely related to those of a speaking voice, in rhythm also the cadence and timing of speech override other musical or poetic factors. As Irish musicologist Seán O'Boyle has written:

> Whilst a *sean-nós* singer reflects the stresses of a poetic metre in his performance, he does not feel bound to observe the isochronous nature of the metrical feet. Being involved in the atmosphere and meaning of the song, he moves from stress to stress at his own pace which is really dictated by the feeling he puts into the words and by the amount of ornamentation and the number of stops he chooses to use in his gracing or "humouring" of a tune (O'Boyle 1976, 17).

Every performance of a *sean-nós* song is a kind of collaboration between the present singer and past generations of singers, poets, and composers. Melodies and lyrics change, not only from singer to singer, but even in different performances by the same person. Did Creggan Graveyard's composer sing the same tune in the eighteenth century that Pádraigín sings today? We cannot know. *Sean-nós* singers learn melodies by ear, not from written notation, guaranteeing that songs change over time.

While we don't know how Art McCooey meant "Creggan Graveyard" to be sung, we can examine how the melody interacts with the words in a contemporary performance. In Pádraigín's singing of "Creggan Graveyard," the music follows the four-line structure of the poetry, labeled as lines A, B, C, and D in the text just presented. The contour of the melody seems to reinforce the meaning of the text. In line B, the highest note renders the word *maidne*, "daybreak" in the translation. Line C is musically identical to line A, except for its final notes; the lower ending note in line C calls special attention to the words *mar ór* ("like gold"), which describe the hair of the young woman in the poet's vision. In line D, the highest notes correspond to the words *íocshláinte an domhain*, the "cure" for the world's ills.

In terms of rhythm, Pádraigín sings freely, adding pauses and elongating or shortening notes to reflect the meaning and emotion of the words. Line B ends with a pause, providing a breathing space for both the singer and the listeners, who require time to absorb its impact. Line C has already been noted because of the way its melody diverges from that of line A to set off the words *mar ór* ("like gold"); rhythmically also, these syllables require an extra beat, and are followed by a rest, lending them added emphasis. Finally, the deceleration at the end of line D acts to mark the end of the verse.

A SINGER'S MISSION

Pádraigín Ní Uallacháin became familiar with the melody of "Creggan Graveyard" through a recording of the piper Séamus Ennis, who played it instrumentally as a slow air. Ennis had learned the air from a cylinder recording of a singer named Mary Harvessy, recorded near the year 1900. Pádraigín sought out the original recording, to find the source

FIGURE 6.2 *Pádraigín Ní Uallacháin.* *(Used with permission from Pádraigín Ní Uallacháin)*

of Ennis's inspiration. She regards this kind of work—researching, reconstructing, singing, recording, and publishing old songs from the Gaelic singing tradition of South Armagh—as her life's mission. Pádraigín inherited this mission from her father, Pádraig Ó hUallacháin. Although he was born in English-speaking County Louth, from age fourteen onwards Ó hUallacháin spent his summers studying Irish Gaelic in the Donegal *gaeltacht*, in a college founded by linguist-researcher Lorcán Ó Muirí. Inspired by Ó Muirí's enthusiasm for the Irish language and *sean-nós* singing, Ó hUallacháin himself became a song collector, passing his love of the tradition on to Pádraigín. She recalls:

My first language was Irish. Music, there was always music in the house. My father was very interested in songs, and we always sang in the car, we always sang at home. There was an emphasis as well on composing songs . . . My father was a very fine singer of *sean-nós* songs . . .

I remember the very first *sean-nós* song that I heard, when I was about seven—that made an impact on me . . . And in later years, he would talk about singers, and he would say they didn't have the *sean-nós*, so that he obviously had come in contact with what the *sean-nós* was . . .

He did apply as a school inspector to be sent to the *gaeltacht*, so that he could bring us up in the *gaeltacht*, and he was denied that . . . so he was keen that we *would* live in the *gaeltacht*. He recognized the importance of the community as being the primary source, as well as the family, for the acquisition of language. But we never lived in the Irish-speaking areas (Ní Uallacháin in discussion with authors, 2001).

Pádraigín's parents met at the Irish college in Donegal, and raised their eight children as Irish speakers. Both parents were musical; her mother had learned the fiddle as a teenager. In school, Pádraigín learned music from outside the *sean-nós* tradition: choir singing, musicals, and piano. Then, as a young woman, she followed her father's example, seeking out traditional singers in the *gaeltacht*:

When I was about nineteen or twenty I spent a lot of time in Connemara. I heard Máire Áine Ní Dhonnchadha, I knew Seosamh Ó hÉanaí (Joe Heaney) well. Then I met a lot of northern singers, in my early twenties—like Len Graham, Joe Holmes, Eddie Butcher. *All* of those singers influence a singer. And then you create your own style— I believe, my style would be very Ulster . . .

I was listening . . . I would listen, and then I would go and buy—
all my first salaries would have been spent on recordings, and then
I'd end up pawning them all and starting all over again . . .
There was a period when I would be listening so much to others
and saying, "what exactly were they doing with ornamentation?" And
then there comes a point when this comes spontaneously, and knits
together with the expression of emotion and feeling. And then you
let the song take off on its own . . .
I spent a long period listening rather than singing out . . . I was
listening a lot, an awful lot, over the period, and singing a lot on my
own. But only very occasionally would I feel that I was of that standard that should sing out . . .
I think singing generally is a solitary activity. It's at its *healthiest*
when it's community-based. . . . The singing in Connemara, a lot of
it is community-based, but I'd say that's probably the exception to
most places in Ireland. In Connemara, you can learn a song, you could
go out on Saturday night, and you could have an audience that night,
if you're standing at the bar, somebody could call you to sing, regardless of what's happening in the pub . . . I would *never* have that
experience. I could learn a *hundred* songs, that some of them may *never*
see the light of day, unless I record them . . . It would be strange for
me to now live in a community where either my language or my
singing was an intrinsic part of the community around me. It would
be certainly a bonus, maybe in my next life, but—it is a solitary
activity . . .
I would say most of the singing that I heard was in pubs, or informally, or unplanned. Late at night, early hours of the morning . . .
probably heard the best singing that I ever heard would be three, four
'o clock in the morning. That would be the main context. I never liked
going to concerts to listen to *sean-nós* singing. I think it was always
the wrong context (ibid.).

After Pádraigín began singing out in late night pub sessions, she
began performing on the stage, but she still finds this to be an un-
comfortable context for *sean-nós* singing. Interestingly, she performs
in collaboration with jazz musicians in Scandinavia, where she
feels that audiences are more receptive to *sean-nós* than audiences in
Ireland:

Where I find myself performing in Norway and in Denmark, Scandinavia, the audience who come are only interested in the expression
of feeling, so what comes across is what impacts, regardless of lan-

guage. And that appeals to me, because maybe that's where my strength is, in the expression of feeling and emotion . . .
There isn't a big audience for *sean-nós* singing in Ireland. It comes back to the question of language, and ease. There's a discomfort because people feel they *ought* to understand; if they'd only relax and sit back and *feel*, they would understand, but they feel, because they haven't got the language, or they left the language aside, or the language was just a school subject, that they're cut off in some way, and the barriers are down (ibid.).

In collaboration with other musicians, Pádraigín has made several recordings of songs to introduce new singers and listeners to the tradition. Her latest and most ambitious recording and publishing project is entitled *Songs from a Hidden Ulster* (2003), a collection of fifty-four songs from South Armagh. Research for this project involved years seeking out the surviving song texts, searching through the available recordings and notation to "remarry" the lyrics with their melodies, and piecing together biographies of the singers and collectors who served as her sources. She describes her mission to pass these songs on to future generations:

I felt a responsibility, as well as an interest, to leave behind, when it comes to my time to move on, a body of work in the area in which I live, so that somebody, even if it's only *one* person that comes after me who wants to sing, will have a source of the material that was vibrant at one stage in the area in which I lived.
Because in cosmic time it's such a short space of time that the language has died; it's only a matter of a generation or two, but the songs *were* there, so my publishing project is to leave, primarily a sense of responsibility to all those who've worked before me, and to the carriers of the song tradition. In fact, I feel in a way that I don't really have any choice but to do this work . . . I love the work and I'm very interested and enthusiastic about it, but I feel a tremendous responsibility, because they lost the language, to leave that body of work behind, so that somebody else can take it a step further (ibid.).

Thanks to the work of singers and researchers like Pádraigín Ní Ualacháin and support from governmental, educational and media institutions devoted to the promotion of the Irish language, Irish Gaelic song has survived into the twenty-first century, and is enjoying somewhat of a resurgence among lovers of traditional music. The next section focuses on similar processes of song-collecting and cultural renewal in the English-language singing of Len Graham.

A LINGUISTIC MEETING-GROUND: IRISH TRADITIONAL SONGS IN ENGLISH

Broadly speaking, Irish traditional songs in English include: (1) Gaelic songs translated into English, (2) English and Scottish ballads brought to Ireland by soldiers, English and Scottish colonists, and migrant Irish laborers traveling between England, Scotland, and Ireland, and (3) English language songs composed by Irish authors.

The exchange of songs between England and Ireland accelerated in the seventeenth century, when the Crown increased its military presence in Ireland and established large "plantations" of English and Scottish settlers, especially in northern Ireland. Plantation and intermarriage led to the importing of many English-language ballads, which gradually absorbed Irish influence through the substitution of Irish airs for English melodies and the adoption of musical and poetic usages from Irish song.

Many indigenous English language songs were composed by "hedge schoolmasters." After the 1310 Statute of Kilkenny, the education of native Irish was discouraged or banned by a succession of British laws. In the eighteenth century, this ban stimulated the widespread creation of secret "hedge schools," in which Irish pupils received instruction in a broad range of subjects. The hedge schoolmasters frequently were poets and singers, and they created a large body of songs, characterized by the use (in English) of Gaelic assonance and meter, classical and Biblical allusions, and flowery poetry.

As the Irish language lost ground across the country, the employment of Gaelic poetic devices in English lost sway, but new songs in English still presented Irish stories and sentiments viewed from an Irish perspective. Narrative songs in English reached their heyday in the nineteenth century, when itinerant ballad singers sold lyric sheets at markets, fairs, athletic events, and political meetings. These ballads addressed a broad range of issues including love, emigration, forced conscription into the British army, murders, shipwrecks, and the execution and banishment of Irish heroes.

The nineteenth century also gave rise to a new genre of genteel "folk songs," which originated not with "the folk" but with collectors and composers who either sanitized existing repertoire or created new songs in imitation of folk models. Thomas Moore dominated the style (see Chapter 2). Irish musicologist Seán O'Boyle described the genre in this way:

> Moore's songs were nostalgic, pseudo-historical, whimsical, sentimental productions suited to the drawing rooms of the nineteenth

century, and were in striking contrast to the live Gaelic love-songs, lullabies, *aislingí* (vision poems) laments, drinking songs, hymns and work-songs of the Irish-speaking people (O'Boyle 1976, 13–14).

In song, as in instrumental music, much Irish repertoire traveled to America with emigrants over the last two centuries. Irish song collectors often consult American publications and singers to recover songs that left Ireland in past generations and have not survived in their place of origin. Listen now to one such example, CD track 24: "Love Won't You Marry Me," a song that Irish singer Len Graham "retrieved" in 1990 from John Ward, an Irish-American singer, then in his late eighties, who learned it from his father who had brought it from Donegal.

Love Won't You Marry Me
I'm tired now of single life,
My mind's made up to take a wife,
To help me through this world of strife,
And to keep me out a' danger.

Chorus:
Love won't you marry me, oh marry me, marry me,
Love won't you marry me and keep me out a' danger?
Love won't you marry me, oh marry me, marry me,
Love won't you marry me and keep me out a' danger?

I have a cottage by the sea,
Adorned with flowers for her and me,
And any girl would happy be,
And I would treat her fairly.

(Chorus)

And now that we the knot have tied,
And she for years has been my bride,
Wi' lots a' children by our side,
We're shielded from all danger.

(Chorus)

[Lilted section (dance tune)]:
Ridle um diddlye dee iydle diddlye deedle
Um diddley die, rattle diddle dee diedoh
Rum diddledee dum diddlye dee iydle diddlye deedle
Um diddley die, rattle diddle dee daydoh . . .

The three verses and chorus of "Love Won't You Marry Me" give lighthearted expression to important values in the remote agricultural society and economy of the extreme north of Ireland: love, marriage, family, and fertility. "Danger," for a young single farmer in Donegal, meant isolation: the lack of a wife to provide companionship and help in the home, and the lack of offspring to provide hands to work the land. "Lots of children by our side" provided an important "shield" from the danger of being alone.

The texted song is followed by a "lilted" dance tune. Lilting refers to the singing of Irish dance tunes to vocables, syllables which have no literal meaning, and is analogous to many vocal traditions around the world, such as scat singing in jazz or *tarana* singing in north India. Many Irish musicians attribute the origin of lilting to the scarcity of affordable instruments in rural Ireland, or to the difficulty of getting instruments repaired. Lilters would be called into service to provide music for dancing when no instruments or players were available. Lilting continues to play an important role in learning music; musicians sometimes lilt a tune before attempting to play it, or to remind one another of tunes. Lilting has also become a performance art in its own right, and lilting competitions are held each year by CCÉ (Madden 1999, 214–6).

ACTIVITY 6.2 *Learn by ear to sing the verses, chorus, and lilted dance tune of "Love Won't You Marry Me."*

A Floating Repertoire of Tunes and Verses. In English as in Gaelic, much of the Irish song repertoire is lyrical rather than narrative. The audience is assumed to be in possession of any story line essential to the understanding of a song, either by virtue of its being common knowledge, or because the singer has presented it in a spoken prologue. For this reason, verses and melodies tend to float from song to song, reassembled from singer to singer and performance to performance. The logic of such performances is circular rather than linear; verses move *around* the subject, presenting it from different poetic angles, rather than presenting it in a step by step, chronological fashion (O'Rourke 1985, 13).

Nineteenth century ballad sheets, and Irish song collections dating into the late twentieth century, frequently presented only the words of a song, assuming that singers would fit the lyrics to a traditional tune of their own choosing. To provide an example, Len Graham has sung the initial verses of "The Banks of the Bann" to two different melodies. The first he heard from an old recording of singer Richard Hayward, and later from Len's good friend Eddie Butcher. Len heard the second melody from singers Malachy Clarkson and Mick Hoy, and has recorded the entire song to this air on his CD *Do Me Justice.* Listen to the two selections on CD tracks 25 and 26 while reading the lyrics:

The Banks of the Bann
When first to this country I came as a stranger,
I placed my affection on a maid that was young.
She being young and tender, her waist small and slender,
Kind affection has made her to be my overthrow.

On the banks of Bann Water where first I beheld her,
She appeared like a goddess or like some Grecian queen.
Her eyes shone like diamonds, her hair bright and golden,
Kind affection has made her to be my overthrow.

Now let me try the other version of it . . .

When first to this country, I came as a stranger,
I placed my affection on a maid that was young.
She being young and tender, her waist small and slender,
Kind affection has made her to be my overthrow.

On the banks of Bann Water, where first I beheld her,
She appeared like a goddess or like some Grecian queen.
Her eyes shone like diamonds, and her hair bright and golden,
Her cheeks like to roses, or like blood drops on snow.

'Twas her cruel parents, I must blame for this variance,
Because I was poor and of a low degree.
But I'll do my endeavors, for to gain my love's favor,
Although she is come of a rich family.

Linguistically, these verses illustrate the use of a floating stock of lines, verses, and images that move from song to song. "She being young and tender, her waist small and slender," "She appeared like a goddess or like some Grecian queen," "Her cheeks like to roses, or like blood drops on snow," and "her cruel parents" appear in many songs, and the theme of a young suitor who is rejected for being too poor is common in American, English, and Irish folk songs.

FIGURE 6.3   Cover art of Do me Justice.   (From "A Broadsheet" by Jack Butler Yeats, by kind permission of the University of Reading. Permission given by Len Graham.)

Compare the melodies while listening again to the two versions. Version one is sung smoothly in triple meter, in the key of D major. The ornamentation consists almost entirely of single grace notes sliding up or down into a main melody note. The melody is in four distinct parts (ABCD) corresponding to the four lines of text.

Version two presents more challenges to the listener. It is sung in a drawn-out fashion, with many extended notes and pauses. At times it seems to be in the key of A major, but G natural (the flatted seventh) and even C natural (the flatted third) make striking appearances, giving the air a very "modal" feeling. It is highly ornamented. Indeed, the

FIGURE 6.4 *Two versions of "The Banks of the Bann."*

FIGURE 6.5   *Len Graham.*   *(Used with permission from Len Graham)*

two melodies seem to represent two distinct kinds of Irish traditional tunes: one fitting easily into the major/minor tradition of modern European melody, and the other representing a distinct (and perhaps older), modal, melismatic tradition. Finally, version two uses its complete melody twice in rendering a single verse (ABAB).

Len Graham: "A Compulsive Singer."   Like his wife, Pádraigín Ní Uallacháin, Len Graham (b. 1944) is a major performer, collector, and publisher of Irish traditional songs, and he is one of very few full-time professional traditional singers in Ireland. Born into a musical family in Glenarm, in Northern Ireland, he seems almost to have been born singing:

> [My] very earliest recollections are of singing, and *me* singing. My mother used to say that I was singing before I could talk, and cer-

tainly my very earliest memories are of singing. I seem to have got the bug very, very early, because they couldn't keep me quiet. I was constantly singing and always seemed to be at that, and my father was a singer, my mother was a singer, my grandparents—seemed to be a lot of music about, and as I say, I don't remember doing anything else but singing. As Pádraigín will tell you, I'm a compulsive singer; I have to sing every day, whether it's to myself or whatever—it just is something that I *have* to do (Graham in discussion with authors, 2001).

Len's mother, Eveline Robinson, provided the model for his "compulsive," everyday singing; they often sang together around the house, not only traditional songs from their area in the Glens of Antrim, but also "whatever'd be comin' out of the radio." His father, Samuel Graham, did more public singing, either in pubs, or occasionally in variety shows, beginning with benefit concerts for the Red Cross during World War II. Len began singing in public in his early teens; his father would sit in the audience, coaching and encouraging him.

I remember singing at a concert that he was in the audience, and where I came down very upset, because the people before me and the people after me were doin' sort of comedy acts and got much more response than what I [got], you know—He said to me, "That's the nature of what you're at, you know; if you get through to *one* person out there in that audience you're providing a service. Don't expect," he says, "to get the same response as the funny person, or the comedy act." (ibid.)

Each summer, the Grahams would visit relatives in Scotland, where at age eleven Len acquired a taste for the late hours of a singer's life—and enjoyed the rewards of singing for pay:

We used to go across to relatives over in Scotland, and this was a good place to perform, because there was the incentive of money. If you did your party piece at some of these gatherings—family gatherings over in Scotland, on our holidays—then you got a chance of performing, and if you did perform, there was a few shillings in it for you as well. And you were also like, stayin' up very late, this was another thing: that you, three o'clock in the morning you were still out of your beds and gettin' paid for singin' a couple of songs, you know? (ibid.)

During his early teens, Len found an outlet for singing in the Scouts. The compulsive nature of his vocalizing sometimes provoked unexpected responses:

> In the Scouts there was a sort of a campfire singaround, and you did your party piece, so again, like I used to be always singin'. And [I] remember going out to one camp, over Scotland again . . . We sailed from Belfast to Glasgow, overnight sailing, and they couldn't shut me up, and they tied a scarf around my mouth to shut me up, you know (ibid.).

In 1963, Len began attending CCÉ English language singing competitions, ultimately winning first prize in 1971. He also went with his father to Antrim-Derry fiddlers' nights, where in 1963 he met an older singer named Joe Holmes, who was to become Len's first regular singing partner.

> He came over; actually I was singing at one of those Antrim and Derry fiddlers' nights. I was asked to sing, and Joe came over to me and asked me for one of the songs that I'd got from my grandmother—it was a song that his, I don't think his mother sang but his grandmother sang . . .
> So he asked me for it, and I came around to his house shortly after that. He started singin' for me. Nobody had told me that he sang, and he hadn't sung for years, you know? He was known as a fiddler. In the Antrim and Derry fiddlers, I was always askin' who would sing, and who didn't sing—but nobody ever associated Joe with singin' . . . Very shortly after that, actually, we started singin' out a bit, singin' together and going around (ibid.).

Len Graham and Joe Holmes remained close friends until the latter's death in 1978.

For many years, Len traveled at least once a week to swap songs with another older singer with a great collection of songs: Eddie Butcher of Magilligan, in north Derry. Len was inspired to seek out Eddie Butcher while hearing a broadcast of Eddie's singing on the radio, in a show produced by the eminent song collector Hugh Shields.

> I'll tell you how it happened. There was a radio program that Hugh Shields did . . . and I happened to be listening to the radio and I heard this singer, in Magilligan. [I] jumped in the car—and drove off to Magilligan. Of course I was living in Ballymoney, which is twenty miles from Magilligan; it wasn't a million miles away. And landed in Magilligan, asked where Eddie Butcher lived and somebody di-

rected me, and [I] rapped the door and Gracie Butcher opened the door and I said "was Eddie Butcher on the radio?"

So I just landed within an hour at their house, from him bein' on the radio. And started up a friendship . . . and then the following time I took Joe Holmes with me. I said, "Can I bring a friend?" to Eddie and Gracie. So, "Of course," and I brought Joe down, and then we kept this up from the late '60s to the late '70s when Joe died, in '78. And I kept going, until Eddie died in 1980. And if for some reason or another I didn't manage to get down there, the phone woulda' rung, and [Eddie] said "Have I done something to you? Why have you not come down to sing for me?" And as soon as I brought Pádraigín down, the first thing he says is, "Can she sing?" And he had her singin' (ibid.).

Pádraigín recalls that she would learn a new song in English every week to sing for Eddie, "cause there's no point in singing in Irish for him." Eddie Butcher's home was the site of many *céilís*, which in Northern Ireland refers not only to dances but to informal entertainment including songs and stories. Pádraigín describes the Butcher household as "the last *céilíng* house, I'd say, certainly in Ulster."

We noted that sessions at the Góilín Singers' Club demonstrate the principles of hospitality, generosity, reciprocity, inclusiveness and exclusiveness, which seem to permeate the social life of Irish traditional music. We again observe these features as Len and Pádraigín describe a typical *céilí* with Eddie and Gracie Butcher:

LEN: Well initially, it would have been to the pub first; we'd have gone to the local pub, and at that time, in the '60s, there were quite a lot of singers around Magilligan, in that generation, Eddie's generation, although Eddie would have been recognized as bein' the main one. His brother John was still singin' at that time, but he wouldn't have the repertoire that Eddie would have had. He had an enormous repertoire—hundreds of songs, you know? John would have had maybe a dozen songs, but sang them very, very well. And there would have been a lot of singers of that generation still alive that would have met in the local pub, Greta Deegan's, and woulda' been great singarounds. But then that sorta' died out; a lot of these singers started dying off, and the pub became noisy, and the younger generation seemed to be moving in, and we stopped going to the pub and we just would have gone to Eddie's house.

PÁDRAIGÍN: Arriving about nine—

LEN: Around nine o'clock, and usually brought a carry-out with us, and would have had a few—

PÁDRAIGÍN: Eddie would start to sing, straightaway—

LEN: Straightaway, yeah. It would have been straight, there'd have been no niceties, or—

PÁDRAIGÍN: Sat in the same chair—

LEN: He never budged, it was always Gracie woulda' ha', probably about eleven or midnight she woulda' came up with the sandwiches and tea—

PÁDRAIGÍN: *Heaps* of sandwiches.

LEN: So, that would have gone on till the early hours of the morning.

PÁDRAIGÍN: We'd leave about—they were *old*, at the time—we would leave about—two?

LEN: And sometimes later (Graham and Ní Uallacháin in discussion with authors, 2001).

Hospitality and generosity appear in the welcome and sandwiches offered by Eddie and Gracie, reciprocity in the "carry-out" (usually Guinness stout) brought by Len and Pádraigín, and exclusiveness in the eventual decision to avoid singing in the increasingly noisy pub. Inclusiveness is manifest in the invitation for Joe Holmes and Pádraigín to join the sessions, and in "the easy interreligious mix in these Northern Irish gatherings (Joe and Len were Protestant and the others Catholic). Such camaraderie among singers and musicians [of the two faiths] has long existed and continues to do so." (Munnelly 2003) These *céilís* continued until 1980, when Eddie Butcher died as he had lived, learning a song jotted on a piece of paper that Len had just produced from his pocket.

The deaths of Joe Holmes and Eddie Butcher created a vacuum in Len Graham's musical life, as Pádraigín recounts:

Len was working in an industrial plant . . . And they started to cut back on the work force, and doubling the work of the official workers, who were learning songs underneath the desk. And I saw Len, being a compulsive singer, who had lost Joe, lost Eddie—he'd actually no outlet anymore. And he used to walk around the fields singing. Next door to our house. He was walking around the field all the time. And he started doing night duty, which was disastrous for everything. And I remember thinking, "how can we improve on this?" (Ní Uallacháin in discussion with authors, 2001)

Improving on the situation involved several steps: Pádraigín became a teacher, and Len quit his plant job to become a full-time performer, giving concerts and recording several albums, both solo and with his newly formed band "Skylark." The audience for unaccompanied singing was small, so professional touring meant collaborating with instrumentalists to provide accompaniment for Len's traditional repertoire. Like many contemporary musicians, Len enjoyed the challenge of creating ensemble arrangements of his songs, but purists within the folk "establishment" could be critical of such changes within the tradition. Pádraigín describes the dilemma:

> . . . When he [Len] went professional, he would have to sing with a band and accompaniment to make a living. That affects the tradition of unaccompanied singing in a way. There's two things: first of all, you *enjoy* singing with accompaniment, but there's also that you *have* to in order to make a living, because you could never make a living if you didn't diversify . . . But . . . you're left so open to criticism for doing that, for singing with accompaniment. But the people who are criticizing would be happy that he walked around the field for the rest of his days and preserved the tradition. Nobody'd hear, but the tradition was preserved! (ibid.)

CONCLUSION

If we take the term *sean-nós* broadly, to mean the old styles of Irish unaccompanied singing in both Irish and English, how is the *sean-nós* managing to survive in twenty-first century Ireland? In singing clubs like the Góilín, and in the performing of singers like Pádraigín Ní Uallacháin and Len Graham, the answer is that the old styles survive by being brought into new musical contexts. For Len Graham, and for the thousands of listeners who have encountered the repertoire of singers like Joe Holmes and Eddie Butcher through his music, the change has involved moving the songs from intimate *céilís* among a handful of friends to public concerts, and to the even less intimate media of CDs and cassette tapes. For Pádraigín Ní Uallacháin, new contexts include not only concert halls and recordings, but also jazz concerts in Scandinavia. Both Len and Pádraigín have recontextualized their songs by performing with accompaniment.

We will conclude this chapter by considering the trajectory of one particularly old song into the contemporary repertoire. Folklorist Tom Munnelly recorded the songs of the Irish traveler John Reilly in 1968. The "travelers" (formerly called "tinkers") have produced many of Ireland's finest musicians up to the present, but as a group they are subject to wide distrust and a certain amount of persecution. The term "tinker," now regarded as pejorative, originally described their occupation as tinsmiths, a viable profession before the advent of plastic. Tom Munnelly recalls that John Reilly

> used to say of himself, "I'm a tinker, and a good one." And he was, because for many years afterwards, the pots he made, the tin cans, the little pails for milking cattle—he used to make tin ornaments as well. Plastic hadn't taken over farm implements, so you would get your pots repaired by the traveling tinker, by the tinsmith, and you would certainly buy all your tins, your tin ware. And, as I say, plastic hadn't replaced them there, so there was a comparative welcome, as artisans, to travelers in and around the countryside, up to the '60s (Munnelly in discussion with authors, 2001).

One of the songs which Tom Munnelly recorded from John Reilly was "The Well Below the Valley," an eerie ballad which seemed to have disappeared after a version of it was published by Francis Child in the nineteenth century. This extraordinary song captured the attention not only of folklorists, but of singer Christy Moore, who subsequently recorded the song with the group Planxty. Tom Munnelly remembers that

> Christy Moore heard John sing a few times. I don't think he ever actually recorded him himself, but I managed to give him recordings, and he's included a good number of the songs in his repertoire: "Raggle Taggle Gypsies," "Lord Bateman," and "The Well Below the Valley."
>
> I've always thought that Christy treated the songs that he got with respect; people have asked me, you know, "Does it not worry you, that it became almost a hit?" As far as I'm concerned, there's a song that was hanging on by the merest thread, from medieval times, and if there are now thousands of people who know it, and hundreds of people maybe who have it in their repertoire, nationally and internationally, I mean—well and good! Songs, they are meant to survive on the lips of the people, not be be put away in bank vaults (ibid.).

CHAPTER 7

Irish Music in the Global Marketplace

During the last forty years, the intimate world of house parties among family, friends and neighbors has given way to more public settings for singing and playing music. For musicians who have grown up or encountered music in more traditional contexts, performing Irish music today involves important aesthetic choices, balancing respect for the tradition against individual creativity and, for professionals, the need to make a living as a performer.

The dynamism of Irish music today is reflected in the many paths that musicians take in their approach to its performance. Contemporary performers range from purists, who want to preserve repertory and performance styles of the past, to modernizers creating syntheses that incorporate aspects of Irish traditional music in rock, rap, and other popular genres. Some are composers, such as the Chicago born fiddler Liz Carroll, whose new tunes fit into traditional forms. Many musicians wear multiple hats, depending on their circumstances and interests. For example, Pádraigín Ní Uallacháin and Len Graham are dedicated researchers and preservationists deeply involved with the community of traditional singers, and at the same time are innovators and professional performers, bringing their arrangements of songs into new contexts. Fiddler Martin Hayes seems equally at home as a member of the Tulla Céilí Band, playing tunes in the East Clare style of his father P. J. Hayes, or performing his own unique and virtuosic tune renditions on stage.

One of the main shifts in performance practice since the 1960s has involved the addition of accompaniment to songs, dance tunes, and slow airs. This change came about partly through the influence of the British and American folk revivals and partly through the work of several key musicians and groups—the Clancy Brothers and Tommy Makem, Seán Ó Riada, and the Chieftains. Makem and the Clancy Brothers sang traditional Irish ballads in a sing-along style, accompanying themselves on guitars and banjo. Based in New York, the group's style was influenced by the American folk music of the period, especially by the banjo picking of Pete Seeger and the vocal harmonies of his group, The Weavers. The group's appearance on the Ed Sullivan show in 1961 launched them as international stars, spawning a new style back in Ireland called "ballad singing," and inspiring a host of groups including the Dubliners and the Wolf-Tones (O'Connor 2001, 102–106). Their songs, such as the ones recorded on their famous 1959 recording, *The Rising of the Moon: Irish Songs of Rebellion*, were sung in households and pubs throughout the Irish diaspora.

The Chieftains experimented with harmony and texture in their renditions of traditional dance tunes and songs. The group grew out of an earlier ensemble led by Seán Ó Riada (1931–1971), a prolific composer, music director at the Abbey Theater, radio broadcaster, and professor of music at University College Cork. His group, Ceoltóirí Chualann, was formed with traditional players and singers for a performance at the Abbey in 1959. Critical of the *céilí* band sound in which all the melody instruments played in unison throughout a whole tune, he began to experiment with texture, alternating between different instrumental combinations and solos. He also pioneered the use of harmony and introduced new instruments into the traditional ensemble—the harpsichord and the *bodhrán*.

Ó Riada's work had a profound effect on the direction of Irish traditional music. Many traditional musicians continue to explore ideas he initiated in the use of accompaniment and arrangements. Ó Riada's immersion in the cultural life of the Irish speaking area of west Cork also helped to revitalize musical traditions in the Gaeltacht, and his teaching at University College Cork gave traditional music an important role in an academic environment for the first time (O'Connor 2001, 74–83). His compositions and arrangements of traditional Irish music for orchestra and choir created new bridges between European art music, religious music, Anglo-American folk music, and Irish traditional music.

Mícheál Ó Súilleabháin (b. 1950) is an important contemporary composer who was influenced by Ó Riada's legacy. Trained as a classical pianist and ethnomusicologist, Ó Súilleabháin has composed many scores integrating Irish traditional music with classical music and jazz. He founded the Irish World Music Centre at the University of Limerick in 1994, a graduate program designed to incorporate the study of Irish traditional music with other world music traditions.

FIGURE 7.1 *Micheál Ó Súilleabháin.* *(Reprinted with permission from Micháel Ó Súilleabháin)*

ACTIVITY 7.1 *Listen to the integration of traditional reper-*
toire with jazz style in Micheál Ó'Súilleabháin's variations on
the double jig, "The Old Grey Goose" (CD track 26). In this
piece, he creates a new kind of ensemble by using the piano (usu-
ally used for accompaniment) as a solo instrument, accompanied
by bodhrán. His utilization of syncopation in his left hand and
melodic variations in his right hand create a jazzy feel, but his
use of ornaments and adherence to the melody throughout the
piece—rather than taking solos that leave the original melody
behind—are more traditionally based than jazz-inspired.

While other musicians carried on Ó Riada's work by exploring the
interfaces between Irish traditional music and European art music, the
Chieftains popularized Ó Riada's innovations in traditional music. They
formed in 1963 with three members of Ceoltóirí Chualann (Sean Potts
on tin whistle, Michael Tubridy on flute, and Martin Fay on fiddle),
uilleann piper Paddy Maloney, and *bodhrán* player, Davey Fallon, who
was later replaced by Peadar Mercier. They continued experimenting

with ensemble arrangements, and began touring internationally in the early 1970s as traditional Irish music grew increasingly popular in Europe and the United States. They still perform at major concert halls around the world, and have recorded over fifty albums, collaborated with musicians from many other genres, and been featured in films, radio shows, and on television.

In the 1970s, many groups were inspired by the new "traditional" music style pioneered by the Chieftains and Ceoltóirí Chualann. The two groups with the most influence on audiences and musicians in Ireland, England, and the United States at this time were Planxty and The Bothy Band, whose recordings inspired a whole generation of Irish traditional music devotees, including many non-Irish players in the United States, Canada, and Europe. Both bands included instrumental arrangements and traditional songs with instrumental accompaniment in their concerts and on their albums. Tríona Ní Dhomhnaill, the lead vocalist with the Bothy Band, sang in both Irish and English, while Planxty's Christy Moore, Andy Irvine, and Johnny Moynihan sang solely in English. Planxty's characteristic sound included the rich interplay between Andy Irvine's mandolin and Donal Lunny's bouzouki, as well as Liam O'Flynn's virtuosic *uilleann* piping. The musicians came from a variety

FIGURE 7.2   *Planxty 1978 (L to R): Donal Lunny, Andy Irvine, Matt Molloy (now with the Chieftains), Liam O'Flynn, and Christy Moore.   (Used with permission from Andy Irvine)*

of musical backgrounds, including rock and classical, but all had a strong commitment to finding old repertory, using traditional singers, players, and old recordings and tune collections for their sources. The major developments that emerged from this period include innovative ensemble arrangements, the introduction of new instruments such as the bouzouki and hurdy gurdy, segues in performance from songs to tunes and from one tune type to another, greater use of plectral instruments such as the banjo, guitar, and mandolin, and the use of open tunings on guitars. Andy Irvine's travels in Bulgaria and Romania led Planxty to incorporate Eastern European rhythms and repertoire in their performances and recordings. Both Clannad and the Bothy Band also popularized arrangements of Gaelic songs from Donegal. The more recent band, Altan (led by fiddler and vocalist Mairéad Ní Mhaonaigh) has also drawn much of its repertoire from this region, gathering tunes and songs from family members and local players.

ACTIVITY 7.2 *Listen to Andy Irvine's performance of "Edward Connors," (CD track 8), part of a medley of three emigration songs connected by instrumental breaks from his 1979 solo album, "Rainy Sunday . . . Windy Dreams." Andy is accompanied by fiddler Frankie Gavin, Donal Lunny on guitar and harmonium, and his own bouzouki playing. The arrangement consists of Andy singing over a layered accompaniment, beginning simply with harmonium. The texture builds with the addition of guitar, bouzouki, and finally fiddle. Other cuts on the recording include a song based on the Romanian meter of $\frac{5}{16}$ and a Romanian dance tune.*

RIVERDANCE

There has been a growing trend since the late 1980s to transform elements of the Irish tradition into marketable, modern, syncretic forms. The largest scale phenomena in the "internationalizing" of Irish music and dance were the megashows *Riverdance* and *Lord of the Dance*. Irish music can be seen as a symbol to set the Irish apart, or, more recently, in the case of Riverdance, as a sort of cultural glue to help enact new global syntheses. Although partaking of cultural elements from American popular culture, Riverdance was conceived in Ireland and marketed to an international audience.

The show grew out of a seven minute interlude in the 1994 Eurovision Song Contest, broadcast from Dublin to over three million television viewers in Europe. Producer Moya Doherty commissioned composer and keyboardist Bill Whelan to create a short percussive piece that would showcase Irish dancers, singers, and musicians, using a chorus line. Whelan's previous collaborations with the Dublin based singing group, Anúna, and Spanish and Hungarian musicians, influenced both his composition and his choice of performers for the piece (Smyth 1996, 95–96). Two Irish-American step dance champions—Michael Flatley and Jean Butler—were brought in as the lead dancers.

The huge success of this performance was followed by the Riverdance single hitting the Irish Top Ten as number one within a week and staying there for months. A video was released soon after, becoming the fastest selling video in Irish history (ibid., 35). The success of the single and video inspired Whelan and Doherty to create a full-length show, based on the original choreography and music, but including music and dance from other world traditions. The show opened in 1995 in Dublin with a cast of eighty, including thirty champion Irish step dancers, a large band of traditional Irish musicians, members of Anúna, the Moscow Folk Ballet, the Deliverance Ensemble from Atlanta, Flamenco dancer Maria Page, guitarist Rafael Riquenti, American tap dancers, and Hungarian gaida and kaval player, Nikola Parov.

The show then moved to London, back to Dublin, and the following March to Radio City Music Hall in New York City. By this time, the ninety-eight minute video had sold over 1.5 million copies in Ireland and Great Britain. The phenomenal success of the production led to multiple world tours (see www.riverdance.com).

Riverdance brought elements of traditional Irish culture to mainstream audiences, but in new packages. Female dancers had more freedom with their arm movements and shed their stiff costumes covered with Celtic designs for simple loose miniskirts. The dance was turned into a symbol of power, professionalism, and virtuosity as long lines of dancers pounded out rhythms in perfect unison. The choreography, dance style, and personality of the dancers also led the press to coin the phrase, "Now Irish Dance is Sexy" (Carr 1996, 135). Whelan's music made use of reel and jig forms played on traditional instruments, but was newly composed and highly influenced by Eastern European rhythms.

The show also made use of traditional symbols and themes of Irish life—emigration and nationalism—reversing the ingrained concept of an insular nationalist identity by embracing the perception that Ireland is an important cultural contributor to the world stage (ibid.).

BLACK 47

Riverdance and its successors have brought Irish step dance to the Broadway stage, creating new professional opportunities for step dancers. In a less theatrical realm, performers are exploring the interface between rock, rap and traditional music by juxtaposing traditional instruments, repertoire, and themes with original rock music, instruments, and performance style. This new lineage of rock and punk based Irish bands began with groups like Horslips in the 1970s and Moving Hearts and the Pogues in the 1980s. Some bands import pop/rock elements into Irish traditional music, while others, like the Irish-American band Black 47, incorporate Irish elements into rock, rap, and jazz.

Black 47 performed in a recent Irish festival near Hartford, Connecticut. While on stage, the six male performers projected a decidedly

FIGURE 7.3 *The Riverdance Irish Dance Troupe, Riverdance—The Show.*
(Photo: Joan Marcus; reproduced by kind permission of Abhann Productions.)

dark, urban persona, playing electric guitar, electric bass, drum set, keyboards, trombone, saxophone, and *uilleann* pipes. Irish-born lead vocalist and guitarist Larry Kirwan writes all the material for the group. They opened with the song, "Green Suede Shoes" which alternates rapped lyrics with sections of the reel, "The Flowers of Edinburgh" and instrumental breaks by the trombone player, sax player, and piper. Kirwan's voice was strident and angry, and the snippets of traditional tunes were blasted out in the same way. This juxtaposition of dance tunes within original songs performed in rock, reggae, hip hop, and jazz styles is Black 47's trademark. Kirwan describes this process in the Black 47 website: "Chris (the first piper with the group, Chris Byrne) supplied a legion of jigs, reels, slides, and hornpipes which I barbarized with feedback and boombox beats." (Kirwan 2002).

The group takes its name from the worst year in the Great Famine history: 1847. From the band's start in 1989 in the Bronx, Kirwan's lyrics have been defiantly political, cynical, and confrontational, and the group's logo is a raised shackled fist. He aligned the group with the minority struggle in Northern Ireland, and his songs "Time to Go" and "Fanatic Heart" deal with the conflict. He has also written about famous Irish patriots, the harsh life of Irish emigrants in America, and life on the streets in New York City.

Kirwan positions himself squarely within the long lineage of topical songwriters in Ireland. His songs move from past to present, exploring contemporary and historical issues. At one point in the concert he shouts out, " People ask us why we're political. We say to be Irish is to be political." On the other hand, Kirwan's rendering of decontextualized pieces of tunes or songs breaks from tradition. The group's deconstruction of tunes performed in an aggressive, angry style proclaims Kirwan's belief that traditional forms must be exploded in order to make sense of the past, as well as the present.

NEW DIRECTIONS

Riverdance and Black 47 demonstrate new paths in which Irish music is being refashioned and syncretized on the concert stage. Some feel these developments reveal the adaptability of the tradition, while others view commercializing endeavors as tangential. Nicholas Carolan, Director of the Irish Traditional Music Archive in Dublin, writes:

> In recent decades there have been a number of musical developments that have proved to be both offshoots of the main stem of traditional music and cul-de-sacs from it: the introduction of electric instruments

FIGURE 7.4   *Black 47 (L to R): Thomas Hamlin, Geoffrey Blythe, Andrew Good-sight, Larry Kirwan, Fred Parcells, Chris Byrne.   (Photo courtesy of Shanachie Entertainment)*

. . . the introduction of rock-music styles . . . and the introduction of other ethnic styles of performance . . . The stage show *Riverdance* and its many successors belong to this category. Although enormously popular, they are essentially derivative of recent developments in Irish traditional music and dance rather than belonging to it, and borrow some elements of traditional music for what are otherwise theatrical purposes (Carolan 2000, 25–26).

Flutist Kevin Crawford feels that because Irish traditional music is thriving today, even commercial productions will ultimately lead audiences back to the real roots of the tradition:

Ah, it's savagely healthy I think. I've no fear of it, none! The local scene is flourishing; the international scene is flourishing. There's no major kind of damage. If there is, people are educated enough or knowledgeable enough now to take it or leave it. It's not as if you're going to be brainwashed into listening to a particular brand of Irish traditional music that you don't like . . . And I couldn't even think of anybody who's doing any harm to it at the moment. Even the River-dance experience was brilliant. I think it certainly helped to get the word out there . . . Ultimately what it would have done was draw an audience in, and out of that, a percentage, a number of those will ac-tually go and find what they really like about Irish music, and find out more about it (Crawford in discussion with authors, 2001).

But while he applauds this diversity, he is also very much aware of his own place within the tradition:

Fundamentally what I do is just play very traditional music. I sup-pose I'm extremely conscious of the tradition and I don't like to mess with it too much. I do like change. It's been finding a balance of how do you change something without going totally overboard and mak-ing it sound contrived . . . I don't like to mess with the tune much . . . It's such a precious thing really, the music, you know, it's so impor-tant to me because it's always been essentially what I've done from a very early age. It's not as if I was coming from a different kind of music altogether, like jazz or a really folk-based music and then came into the Irish music and then tried to superimpose what I had known previously into Irish tunes (ibid.).

Kevin's reflexivity about performing traditional music is echoed by Martin Hayes, who tries to balance his audiences' desires, his own cre-ative needs, and the spirit of the music itself in his concerts with gui-tarist Dennis Cahill:

Things are sometimes more clearly understood by direct experience of their opposite. Fast music gives added dimension to slower music and vice-versa, wild passion gives meaning to gentle delicacy. Inno-vation and tradition have a similar relationship. They are mutually inclusive. In concert we try not to exclude any particular aspect of the music. We are always seeking equilibrium between these seemingly opposing perspectives . . . Our primary wish is that the musical ex-perience be one that lifts our spirits and those of the audience. With respect to those aims, we are very fortunate to have access to a body of music that is extremely rich in feeling and emotion. The more I play these tunes, the deeper my respect grows for the music itself (Hayes 1999).

This respect for the integrity of tunes and songs manifests itself differently depending on the musician or band. In trying to find their own identity as a performing group, Kevin's band Lúnasa remains primarily acoustic, but they've created a new sound by using multiple wind instruments and innovative guitar and double bass accompaniments. Their medleys include both traditional tunes and newly composed tunes in traditional forms. Kevin's approaches the new tunes somewhat differently than the traditional ones:

> I don't mind being a little more daring with some of the newly composed tunes. I don't feel that they've been around long enough to merit not being tampered with . . . I know they need to grow, they need to develop, whereas a lot of the really old, traditional tunes, it's very hard to do anything new with them that's going to make them sparkle because chances are that somebody else has already done it because they've been around for hundreds of years. There's probably a definitive version or a definitive recording of that tune that will be never be surpassed. Whereas with a lot of the new tunes, I would take more liberties with them (Crawford in discussion with authors, 2001).

Kevin's decision to play traditional tunes in a straight manner, and experiment with new tunes is based partly on his experience of playing the accompaniment role, even as a flute player. Since accompaniment is a relatively new phenomenon in Irish traditional music, he feels more freedom in creating accompaniment parts:

> The main core, it would always be true to the tune, but we would always try to change things in the way we would layer up a particular sound with harmonies over the genuine or the core melody . . . But I mean I would do things like that when I put myself in a different role. I'm then involved in accompaniment rather than the melody. Again, I don't feel that I'm tampering with anything that way. What I would be doing is filling out, playing out a role within the band just to kind of create or fulfill an arrangement. If I'm playing melody generally I just play the tune as it is. I think that way I can justify to myself that I'm not really messing with anything. I see myself as a guitarist with a flute in my mouth (ibid.).

Innovations also come from unexpected places. While teaching traditional Irish flute at a world music workshop in England, Kevin had the opportunity to hear one of the most well-known exponents of the North Indian bamboo flute, Hari Prasad Chaurasia, who was also giving a workshop. Drawn in by the "haunting, floating, spiritual" sound of Chaurasia's flute, Kevin introduced himself and the two compared their respective instruments and played for each other:

We started exchanging chops, but I remember he used to do this great thing at the time. He would just play a series of notes which wouldn't be anything, it wouldn't be a melody really (demonstrates, repeatedly tonguing one note on his flute). I'd never heard this in Irish music . . . it would be doing a percussive kind of sound from the breath to do with the phrasing. I just instantly thought, if you could adapt some of those ornaments that he has into the Irish flute sound, you would end up having a bit more variation.

So I just started toying around with the triplets with the tonguing . . . Not to overdo it, but just to create a bit of a variant. And the more I became proficient at it like, the more I actually found that it really suited . . . But it's funny how outside influences—going so far off the track for getting ideas for Irish music—it works and it certainly is something that can be in the tradition (ibid.).

Tradition and innovation are closely interwoven in CD track 27, a live recording of Lúnasa performing at the Towne Crier Café in Pawling, New York on July 25, 2003. Kevin raises the issue of modernization in his spoken introduction to this medley, which begins with a traditional reel called "Dr. Gilbert":

It was recorded back in the 1920s by the legendary Michael Coleman. And then we skip about four generations and we come to this young gentleman here, Seán Smyth, and he's still carrying on the tradition with this reel. It's called "Dr. Gilbert," and just to kind of bring it into the twenty-first century, he's playing with Trevor Hutchinson here on the bassitron . . . Michael Coleman didn't have one of these at his disposal when he made the recording in the 1920s, although he did use a piano player that sounded remarkably similar (Crawford 2003).

Kevin's remark on the "similarity" between Hutchinson's "bassitron" and Coleman's piano is facetious; the two are worlds apart. Comparing Lúnasa's performance with Coleman's reveals a great deal about how Irish music has changed (and remained the same) over the last seventy years.

Listen to CD track 9, fiddler Michael Coleman's medley of "Dr. Gilbert" and "The Queen of May," accompanied by Herbert Henry on piano. It is a sprightly performance, with much fiddle ornamentation in the form of triplets and rolls. Both tunes are in ₹, with Coleman giving a pronounced accent to beats one and three. Henry plays a simple

FIGURE 7.5 *Lúnasa (L to R): Donogh Hennessy (guitar), Kevin Crawford (flute and whistles), Cillian Vallely (uilleann pipes and whistles), Séan Smyth (fiddle and whistles), and Trevor Hutchinson (bass).* (Photo by Giorgia Bertazzi, reprinted with permission from Lúnasa)

accompaniment, playing bass notes with his left hand on beats one and three, and block chords with his right on beats two and four. The performance bounces along at around 112 beats per minute, with a lilting, danceable rhythm.

Now listen to Lúnasa's performance on CD track 27. The "bassitron" is an electric upright bass, with a curved bridge that allows the player to play with a bow or pluck with the fingers, and a streamlined body several times thinner than a conventional double bass. The performance begins with Hutchinson bowing a low "E," varying the angle of his bow to create a rich variety of overtones, amplified by the electric pickup to create an otherworldly, space-age ambience. Fiddler Seán Smyth plays "Dr. Gilbert" faster than Michael Coleman, beginning at 126 beats per minute and accelerating from there. His melody is similar to Coleman's, differing in ornamentation within the bounds of traditional style.

Lúnasa plays the tune three times through. In the second verse, the bass rhythm becomes more pronounced, with strong accents on one and three (like the left hand of Coleman's piano player), while guitarist

Donogh Hennessy chunks out a stream of chords, two per beat. In the B section of the tune, both guitar and bass climb stepwise through the first five notes of the scale, two steps per measure, creating an interesting harmonic tension by staying on the fifth scale degree for the second half of the line. In the third verse, Hennessy's guitar places a strong accent on the third beat in each measure, giving the performance a strong "rock" feeling—and creating such rhythmic excitement that the audience begins clapping along.

After the third verse, the bass and guitar drop out as *uilleann* piper Cillian Vallely plays the three-part reel "The Merry Sisters of Fate" in unison with fiddle and flute. This begins as a very traditional performance: pure melody accompanied only by the clapping of the audience. They play the tune four times through, with bass and guitar joining on the last two verses. Guitarist Hennessy accents beats two and four during the third verse (like the right hand of Coleman's pianist); during the fourth verse, he adds rhythmic excitement by delaying his first accent to the second half of the second beat.

The final tune in the medley comes not from Ireland, but was adapted from a suite recorded by Breton guitarist Dan Ar Braz. It is in reel rhythm, but the sections are unequal; the A section consists of a two-measure theme played four times in succession, while the B section is a two-bar phrase played twice. The band plays the tune eight times through, treating it quite freely. On the third and fourth verses, the pipes and flute add high drones and harmonies; on the fifth and sixth verses, they add contrapuntal melodies and counter-rhythms, "riffing" over the basic melody and chord progression. The jazz-like effect recalls Kevin's statement that he doesn't mind being "more daring" with new tunes. As he riffs over the chord progression, he truly plays "like a guitarist with a flute in my mouth."

This performance reveals much that is new in Irish traditional music: a faster tempo, the employment of electric instruments, the use of harmony to transform the feeling of a tune, changes in texture and orchestration, the use of jazz and rock rhythms in accompaniment parts, the adoption of contemporary and non-Irish tunes (in this case, from Celtic Brittany), and jazz-like improvisation over basic tunes and chord progressions. But much is also very traditional: the use of traditional tunes, tune types, and ornamentation, the emphasis on unison melody, the employment of fiddle, wooden flute, and *uilleann* pipes, and the overall atmosphere of energetic, good-humored music making with an infectious danceable rhythm.

CONCLUSION

Throughout its history, the Irish music tradition has been flexible, incorporating a variety of techniques, instruments and styles from other parts of the world, ranging from France, England, and Scotland to America and, more recently, Eastern Europe and India. Influenced by pop music and commercialism within the last forty years, traditional music has also been packaged successfully for the global marketplace, creating new contexts for performance, as well as new hybrid styles. But while change and innovation play a central role in the maintenance of the tradition today, musicians continue to be profoundly influenced by the past. Musicians feel linked both to the rich repertory of songs and tunes and the social world that surrounded performance—the people, places, historic and political events, and way of life that gave life to the music. As Ciaran Carson suggests, the old tunes and songs unite the past and present each time they are performed:

> Each time the song is sung, our notions of it change, and we are changed by it. The words are old. They have been worn into shape by many ears and mouths and have been contemplated often. But every time is new because the time is new, and there is no time like now (Carson 1996, 116).

This understanding of the past informs performance today, especially since the majority of musicians still play in informal sessions where the social aspects of music making play a dominant role. The importance of people and place are embodied in performance style and context. Camaraderie, good humor, respect and love for the music, the elders, and the land, are all values that receive clear expression in traditional contexts for playing and singing. In concerts where the music is performed by professionals for a paying audience, there is often an effort to reenact the sort of humor and intimacy found in a kitchen or pub session. For professional musicians like Kevin Crawford, their participation in small, intimate sessions is often what keeps them inspired about their music:

> It has to be the social side, it has to be the *craic*, the chat, the music, and if you're lucky to get a good bar with a really good listening audience and a bit of atmosphere, you're on a winner. There's no concert that can beat that. We're playing huge audiences around the world. With Lúnasa, thank God, it's going incredibly well, but you're only really giving them a consistent kind of sample of what can hap-

pen in Ireland. I mean the real thing is if you're involved in a great session and if everything is going according to plan, ah my God, you're taken on a different level altogether, which is why I've stayed with music all these years . . . It's something you can't really do without (Crawford in discussion with authors, 2001).

Glossary

Accordion   Member of the free reed instrument family, brought to Ireland by the mid-nineteenth century. Types include the older style ten button melodeon and the button accordion. Piano key accordions were popular in céilí bands, but are less favored in traditional music today.

Aisling (pl. *Aislingí*)   Vision poem, a genre of sean-nós song.

An Coimisiún le Rincí   The Irish Dancing Commission formed in 1929.

Binary form   Musical structure of two different sections (AB); the form of the majority of Irish traditional dance tunes.

Bodhrán   Frame drum consisting of a shallow hoop of wood covered on one side with a stretched skin and reinforced with cross pieces of wood, cord, or wire.

Bouzouki   A Greek long-necked lute, adapted to Irish music in the 1960s.

Céilí (Céilidhe)   (1) In Northern Ireland and older usage, refers to a social visit, visiting, or an evening's entertainment, including conversation, singing, dancing, etc.; (2) More common usage: a social dance event.

Céilí **band**   Musical ensemble originally created to produce a louder sound for accompanying dancers in large venues.

Céilí **dance**   Name given to a group of social dances, some old and some newly composed in the early twentieth century, that were promoted by the Gaelic League as distinctively Irish.

Ceol   Irish term for instrumental music or a session.

Comhaltas Ceoltóirí Éireann **(CCÉ)**   Organization formed in 1952 to promote Irish traditional music and dance and the Irish language.

Concertina   Hexagonal, button operated instrument with bellows, in the same family as the accordion.

Craic   Modern Gaelic term for conversation and fun; derived from the English word "crack" having the same meaning.

Cran   Piping ornament on the lowest note of the chanter.

Cúchulainn   Hero of the eighth century Irish epic, *Táin Bó Cuailnge.*

Cut   Ornament separating two notes of the same pitch by inserting a higher pitch between them.

Dance Halls Act   Passed in 1935 to prohibit informal house or crossroads dances without a license.

Dudeen   Clay pipe.

Feis **(pl.** *Feiseanna***)**   Literally, festival, but involves music and/ or dance competitions.

Feis Ceoil **(***Cheoil***)**   Literally, music festival involving competition; may also include step dancing. The first was held in Dublin in 1897.

Fleadh Cheoil **(pl.** *Fleadhanna***)**   Literally, feast of music. Competition for singers, instrumentalists, and set dancers. The first was held in 1952 as a way to boost the status of traditional music.

Free rhythm   Music without a steady measurable beat; nonmetrical rhythm.

Gaelic League   Organization formed in 1893 to promote Irish nationalism through a revival of the Irish language.

Gaeltacht   Irish speaking areas of Ireland, primarily on the fringes of the country. The Irish language has survived as an unbroken dominant linguistic tradition in these regions and is actively preserved today.

Hornpipe   A dance genre and tune type in duple meter, characterized by the use of dotted rhythms.

Jig   A dance genre or dance tune in compound meter, including the single and double jig in $\frac{6}{8}$, slip jig in $\frac{9}{8}$, and slide in $\frac{12}{8}$.

Lilting   The singing of Irish dance tunes to vocables, syllables that have no literal meaning.

Macaronic   Song in which verses alternate between English and Irish.

Melismatic   Rendering of melody characterized by singing many notes to a single syllable of text.

Melodeon   Early form of the button accordion.

Ornament   Decoration added to a tune or song; types include rolls, cuts, crans, and triplets.

Polka   Dance form in duple meter (typically $\frac{2}{4}$) brought to Ireland in the late 1800s; tunes are most commonly found in Cork, Kerry, and Limerick.

Reel   Solo or group step dance done to music by the same name; popular tune type in duple meter ($\frac{4}{4}$).

Roll   Form of melodic ornamentation; long roll consists of five notes that replace a single dotted quarter note.

Sean-nós   Literally, old style; refers most often to a singing style developed in the Irish language, but also to an "old style" of step dance, associated today with Connemara.

Slow air   Solo instrumental rendition of a song air, often in the *sean-nós* style.

Set dance   Genre of social dance in square formation, originally brought to Ireland by French dancing masters in the nineteenth century.

Slide   Dance tune typically in $\frac{12}{8}$, associated with the Sliabh Luachra region.

Step dance   Virtuosic solo dance where the dancer's feet make percussive patterns on the floor.

Strawboys   Uninvited group of disguised revelers whose appearance at a wedding celebration was thought to bring good luck to the bride and groom.

Syllabic   Rendering of melody by singing one note to each syllable of text.

Triplet   Group of three equal valued notes fit into one beat, often used as a rhythmic and melodic ornament.

Uilleann **pipes**   From the Irish "uillinn" meaning elbow; bellows blown bagpipes consisting of a chanter, three drones, and three regulators. Originally called the Irish union bagipipes.

Waltz   Dance genre and dance tune in triple meter.

References

Boyce, D. George. 1995. *Nationalism in Ireland*. London: Routledge.

Breathnach, Breandán. 1977. *Folk Music and Dances of Ireland*. Dublin: The Mercier Press.

———. 1986. *The Use of Notation in the Transmission of Irish Folk Music*. Cork: The Irish Traditional Music Society.

Brennan, Helen. 2001. *The Story of Irish Dance*. Lanham, Maryland: Roberts Rinehart Publishers.

Brown, Terence. 1985. *Ireland: A Social and Cultural History, 1922 to the Present*. Ithaca: Cornell University Press.

Carolan, Nicholas. 1990. "The Beginnings of the Céilí Dancing: London in the 1890s." Unpublished paper delivered May 19, 1990.

———. 1997. *A Harvest Saved: Francis O'Neill and Irish Music in Chicago*. Cork: Ossian Publications.

———. 2000. "Acoustic and Electric: Irish Traditional Music in the Twentieth Century." *Journal of Music in Ireland*. (Nov/Dec 2000): 20–27.

Carolan, Turlough. 1984. *Complete Collection of the Much Admired Old Irish Tunes*. Cork: Ossian Publications.

Carr, Darrah. 1996. *Irish Dance: Pushing the Boundaries of a Traditional Form*. B.A. thesis, Wesleyan University.

Carson, Ciaran. 1996. *Last Night's Fun*. New York: North Point Press.

Crawford, Kevin. 2001. Interview with authors.

Crehan, Junior. 1973. "Tribute to Willie Clancy" in *Treoir: The Magazine of Irish Traditional Music, Song and Dance*. Uimhir 2, Comhaltas Ceoltóirí Éireann: 8.

Cunningham, Eric. 1999. "Bodhrán" in *The Companion to Irish Music*. Edited by Fintan Vallely. Cork: Cork University Press.

Doherty, Liz. 1999. "Hornpipe" in *The Companion to Irish Music*. Edited by Fintan Vallely. Cork: Cork University Press.

Flood, W. H. Grattan. 1913. *A History of Irish Music*. Dublin: Brown and Nolan. Reprint, New York: Praeger, 1970.

Galvin, Patrick. 2001. Interview with authors.

Gerhard, Joe. 2001. Interview with authors.

Gleeson, Jimmy and Nell. 2001. Interview with authors.

Graham, Len. 2001. Interview with authors.

Hall, Reg. 1995. *The Social Organization of Traditional Music-Making: The Irish in London After the War.* Ó Riada Memorial Lecture 10. Cork: Traditional Music Archive.

Hamilton, Colin. 1999. "Tin Whistle" in *The Companion to Irish Music.* Edited by Fintan Vallely. Cork: Cork University Press.

Hanigan, Steáfán. 1991. *The Bodhrán Book.* Cork: Ossian Publications.

Hayes, Kitty. 2001. Interview with authors.

Hayes, Martin. 1999. Liner notes from *Live in Seattle.* Danbury: Green Linnet Records.

Henigan, Julie. 1999. "Aisling" in *The Companion to Irish Music.* Edited by Fintan Vallely. Cork: Cork University Press.

Heymann, Ann. 1999. "Harp" in *The Companion to Irish Music.* Edited by Fintan Vallely. Cork: Cork University Press.

Hutchinson, John. 1987. *The Dynamics of Cultural Nationalism: The Gaelic Revival and the Creation of the Irish Nation State.* London: Allen and Unwin.

Hobsbawm, Eric. 1983. *The Invention of Tradition.* Cambridge: Cambridge University Press.

Kiberd, Declan. 1989. "Irish Literature and Irish History" in *The Oxford History of Ireland.* Edited by R. F. Foster. Oxford: Oxford University Press.

Kirwan, Larry. 2002. http://www.black47.com.

Mac Con Iomaire, Liam. 1999. "Sean-Nós" in *The Companion to Irish Traditional Music.* Edited by Fintan Vallely. Cork: Cork University Press.

MacNamara, Mary. 2001. Interview with authors.

McCaffrey, Lawrence. 1992. *Textures of Irish America.* Syracuse University Press.

McCarthy, Marie. 1999. *Passing It On: The Transmission of Music in Irish Culture.* Cork: Cork University Press.

Madden, Angela. 1999. "Lilting" in *The Companion to Irish Traditional Music.* Edited by Fintan Vallely. Cork: Cork University Press.

Mercier, Mel. 2002. Interview with Dorothea Hast.

Meyer, Moe. 1995. "Dance and the Politics of Orality: A Study of the Irish Scoil Rince. *Dance Research Journal* 27/1 (Spring 1995): 25–39.

Miller, Kirby A. 1999. "Revenge for Skibbereen": Irish Emigration and the Meaning of the Great Famine" in *The Great Famine and the Irish Diaspora in America.* Edited by Arthur Gribben. Amherst: University of Massachusetts Press.

Moloney, Collette. 2000. *The Irish Music Manuscripts of Edward Bunting (1773–1843).* Dublin: Irish Traditional Music Archives.

Moloney, Mick. 1982. "Irish Ethnic Recordings and the Irish-American

Imagination" in *Ethnic Recordings in America: A Neglected Heritage*. Washington DC: Library of Congress, American Folklife Center.

————. 1999. "Acculturation, Assimilation, and Revitalization: Irish Music in Urban America, 1960–1996" in *Crosbhealach An Cheoil (The Cross Roads Conference) 1996: Tradition and Change in Irish Music*. Edited by Fintan Valleley et al. Cork: Ossian Publications.

————. 1999. "Banjo" in *The Companion to Irish Music*. Edited by Fintan Vallely. Cork: Cork University Press.

Moulden, John. 1994. *Thousands are Sailing: A Brief Song History of Irish Emigration*. Portrush, Co. Antrim: Ulstersongs.

Moylan, Terry, ed. 2000. *The Age of Revolution in the Irish Song Tradition*. Dublin: The Lilliput Press and The Góilín Singers Club.

Munnelly, Tom. 1994. *The Mount Callan Garland: Songs from the Repertoire of Tom Lenihan*. Dublin: Comhairle Bhéaloideras Éireann.

————. 1998. "Junior Crehan of Bonavilla" *Béaloideas* 66 (1998): 59–161.

————. 1999. "Junior Crehan of Bonavilla" (Part Two), *Béaloideas* 67 (1999): 71–124.

————. 2001. Interview with authors.

————. 2003. Written communication with authors.

Newton, Wendy. 2001. Interview with Dorothea Hast.

Ní Uallacháin, Pádraigín. 2001. Interview with authors.

O'Boyle, Seán. 1976. *The Irish Song Tradition*. Cork: Ossian Publications.

Ó Canainn, Tomás. 2002. Interview with Dorothea Hast.

O'Connor, Nuala. 2001. *Bringing It All Back Home*. Dublin: Merlin Publishing.

Ó hAllmhuráin, Gearóid. 1999. "The Great Famine: A Catalyst in Irish Traditional Music Making" in *The Great Famine and the Irish Diaspora in America*. Amherst: University of Massachusetts Press.

O'Henry, Edward. 1989. "Institutions for the Promotion of Indigenous Music: The Case for Ireland's Comhaltas Ceoltóirí Éireann." *Ethnomusicology*: 33–1 (Winter 1989): 67–95.

Ó Muirithe, Diarmuid. 1999. "Song, Macaronic Song" in *The Companion to Irish Traditional Music*. Edited by Fintan Vallely. Cork: Cork University Press.

O'Neill, Francis. 1903. *O'Neill's Music of Ireland*. Chicago: Lyon and Healy.

O'Reilly, Jerry. 2001. Interview with authors.

Ó Rócháin, Muiris. 2001. Interview with authors.

O'Rourke, Brian. 1985. *Blas Maela: A Sip from the Honey Pot*. Dublin: Irish Academic Press Ltd.

————1990. *Pale Rainbow/An Dubh ina Bhán*. Dublin: Irish Academic Press. Ltd.

Ó Súilleabháin, Mícheál. 1984. *The Bodhrán.* Dublin: Department of Irish Folklore, University Colllege.

O'Sullivan, Jerry. 2002. Interview with Dorothea Hast.

Perreten, Sally. 2002. Personal communication with authors.

Schiller, Rina. 2001. *The Lambeg and the Bodhrán.* Belfast: The Institute for Irish Studies, Queen's University.

Sheridan, Ashley. 2000. Interview with Dorothea Hast.

Shields, Hugh. 1993. *Narrative Singing in Ireland.* Dublin: Irish Academic Press.

Simms, Katherine. 1989. "The Norman Invasion and the Gaelic Recovery" in *The Oxford History of Ireland.* Edited by R. F. Foster. Oxford: Oxford University Press.

Sky, Cathy Larson. 1997. *"I'd Barter Them All"—Elements of Change in the Traditional Music of County Clare, Ireland.* M.A. thesis, University of North Carolina, Chapel Hill.

Smyth, Sam. 1996. *Riverdance: The Story.* London: Andre Deutsch.

Takaki, Ronald. 1993. "Emigrants From Erin: Ethnicity and Class within White America" in *A Different Mirror.* Boston: Little, Brown and Company.

Taruskin, Richard. 2000. "Nationalism." *The New Grove Dictionary of Music and Musicians.* Edited by Stanley Sadie. London: MacMillan.

Taylor, Barry. 1984. "The Irish Ceílídh Band—A Break With Tradition?" in *Dal gCais,* #7:67–74.

Tunney, Paddy. 1991. *The Stone Fiddle: My Way to Traditional Song.* Belfast: Appletree Press.

Vallely, Cillian. 2002. Interview with Dorothea Hast.

Vallely, Fintan, ed. 1996. *Crosbhealach An Cheoil (The Cross Roads Conference) 1996: Tradition and Change in Irish Music.* Cork: Ossian Publications.

———. 1999. "Comhaltas Ceoltóirí Éireann (CCÉ)" and "Sean-nós" in *The Companion to Irish Traditional Music.* Edited by Fintan Vallely. Cork: Cork University Press.

Vallely, Niall. 2002. Interview with Dorothea Hast.

Wilkinson, Desi. 2001. Interview with authors.

Wright, William H. A., 1996. *'Twas Only an Irishman's Dream.* Urbana: University of Illinois Press.

Resources

Reading

Cowdery, James. 1990. *The Melodic Tradition of Ireland*. Kent: Kent State University Press.

Curtis, P. J. 1994. *Notes from the Heart*. Dublin: Torc.

Faolin, Turlough. 1983. *Blood on the Harp: Irish Rebel History in Ballad (The Heritage)*. Troy, NY: The Whitston Publishing Company.

Foy, Barry and Rob Adams. 1999. *Field Guide to the Irish Music Session*. Lanham, Maryland: Roberts Rinehart Publishers.

Kearns, Tony and Barry Taylor. 2003. *A Touchstone for the Tradition: The Willie Clancy Summer School*. Kerry, Ireland: Brandon.

Macleod, Karen Ralls. 2003. *Music and the Celtic Otherworld*. Polygon Press.

Melhuish, Martin. 1998. *Celtic Tides: Traditional Music in a New Age*. Kingston, Ontario: Quarry Press. In conjunction with a documentary by the same name, Hallway Productions, Inc.

Moloney, Mick. 2002. *Far from the Shamrock Shore: The Story of Irish-American Immigration through Song*. Cork: Collins Press. Book and CD.

Moylan, Terry, ed. 1994. *Irish Dances*. Dublin: Na Píobairí Uilleann.

Murphy, Pat. 1995. *Toss the Feathers: Irish Set Dancing*. Dublin: Mercier Press.

———. 2000. *The Flowing Tide: More Irish Set Dancing*. Dublin: Mercier Press.

Ní Uallacháin, Pádraigín. 2003. *A Hidden Ulster—People, Songs and Traditions of Oriel*. Dublin: Four Courts Press. http://www.irishsong.com.

Ó Canainn, Tomás. 1993. *Traditional Music in Ireland*. Cork: Ossian Publications.

Ó Riada, Seán. 1982. *Our Musical Heritage*. Portlaoise, Ireland: The Dolmen Press.

Vallely, Fintan and Charlie Pigott. 1998. *Blooming Meadows: The World of Irish Traditional Musicians*. Lanham, Maryland: Roberts Rinehart Publishers.

Wallis, Geoff, et al. 2001. *The Rough Guide to Irish Music*. London: The Rough Guides.

Wilson, David. 1995. *Ireland, A Bicycle and a Tinwhistle*. Montreal: McGill-Queen's University Press.

Zimmerman, Georges Denis. 2002. *Songs of Irish Rebellion*. Dublin: Four Courts Press.

Listening

Altan. 1987. *Frankie Kennedy & Mairéad Ní Mhaonaigh*. Green Linnet Records.

———. 2000. *Another Sky*. Virgin Records.

Black 47. 1993. *Fire of Freedom*. Capitol Records.

———. 1994. *Home of the Brave*. Capitol Records.

Bothy Band. 1993. *1975: The First Album*. Original Release: 1975. Green Linnet Records.

———. 1993. *Old Hag You Have Killed Me*. Original Release: 1976. Green Linnet Records.

Burke, Kevin. 1999. *In Concert*. Green Linnet Records.

Burke, Kevin with Michael Ó Domhnaill. 2001. *Portland*. Original Release: 1982. Green Linnet Records.

Canny, Paddy. 1997. *Paddy Canny: Traditional Music from the Legendary East Clare Fiddler*. MÓC Music LC 4986.

Chieftains. 2000. *Chieftains I*. Original Release: 1965. Atlantic Records.

———. 2002. *Best of the Chieftains*. Atlantic Records.

Clancy Brothers and Tommy Makem. 1998. *The Rising of the Moon: Irish Songs of Rebellion*. London: Tradition Records. http://www.TraditionRecords.com.

Clancy, Willie. 1994. *The Minstrel from Clare*. Green Linnet Records.

———. 1994. *The Pipering of Willie Clancy 1 & 2*. Claddagh Records.

Clannad. 1993. *Banba*. Atlantic Records.

Cran. *Lover's Ghost*. 2000. Black Rose Records. http://www.cran.net.

Crawford, Kevin. 2001. *In Good Company*. Green Linnet Records.

Crehan, Junior, Bobby Casey, Patrick Kelly, and Joe Ryan. *Ceol an Chláir Vol. 1*. Comhaltas Ceoltóirí Éireann CL 17.

Danú. 2002. *All Things Considered*. Shanachie. http://www.danu net.

DeDannan. 1975. *De Dannan*. Polydor Records.

Dennehy, Tim. 1997. *Farewell to Miltown Malbasy*. Sceilig Records SRCD002.

———. 2003. *Between the Mountains and the Sea*. Sceilig Records.

Dervish. 2003. *Spirit*. Compass Records.

Flook. 2002. *Rubai*. Flatfish Records, Worldvillage. http://www.flook.co.uk.

Graham, Len. 1983. *Do Me Justice*. Claddagh Records CC37CD.

———. 1985. *Ye Lovers All*. Claddagh Records Limited.

Graham, Len and Pádraigín Ní Uallacháin. 1996. *When I Was Young*. Gael-Linn.

Hayes, Kitty. 2001. *A Touch of Clare: Traditional Irish Concertina Music*. Clachán Music.

Hayes, Martin. 1993. *Martin Hayes*. Green Linnet Records.

Hayes, Martin with Dennis Cahill. 1999. *Live in Seattle*. Green Linnet Records.

Heaney, Joe. 1996. *Say a Song: Joe Heaney in the Pacific Northwest*. Northwest Folklife and the University of Washington Archives.

Irvine, Andy. 1989. *Rainy Sundays . . . Windy Dreams*. Wundertüte Musik CD TÜT 72.141.

———. 2001. *Way Out Yonder*. Appleseed Records. http://www.Andyirvine. com.

Irvine, Andy and Paul Brady. 1993. *Andy Irvine and Paul Brady*. Original Release: 1976. Green Linnet Records.

Ivers, Eileen. 2002. *Crossing the Bridge*. Sony Music.

Laichtín Naofa Céilí Band. 1960. *An Irish House Party*. Dublin Records LP1007.

Lúnasa. 1999. *Otherworld*. Green Linnet Records. http://www.Lunasa.ie.

———. 2001. *The Merry Sisters of Fate*. Green Linnet Records.

———. 2002. *Lúnasa*. Green Linnet Records.

———. 2003. *Redwood*. Green Linnet Records.

Moylan, Terry, ed. 1994. *Johnny O'Leary of Sliabh Luachra: Dance Music from the Cork-Kerry Border*. Dublin: The Lilliput Press. Tune collection.

Ní Uallacháin, Pádraigín. 1994. *A Stór's A Stóirín*. Gael-Linn CEFCD 166.

———. 1995. *An Dara Craiceann (Beneath the Suface)*. Gael-Linn CEFCD 174.

———. 2002. *An Dealg Óir (The Golden Thorn)*. Gael-Linn CEFCD 183.

O'Leary, Johnny. 1995. *Johnny O'Leary of Sliabh Luachra: Dance Music from the Cork-Kerry Border*. Craft Recordings.

O'Reilly, Jerry. 2003. *Down From Your Pulpits, Down From Your Thrones*. Dublin: Craft Recordings CRCD04.

O'Reilly, Jerry and Terry Moylan (Producers). 2000. *The Croppy's Complaint*. Dublin: Craft Recordings CRCD03.

Ó Súilleabháin, Mícheál. 1995. *Between Worlds*. Venture.

———. 2001. *Templum*. Venture.

O'Sullivan, Jerry. 1987. *The Invasion*. Green Linnet Records.

———. 1998. *The Gift*. Shanachie Records.

Patrick Street. 1999. *Live*. Green Linnet Records.

———. 2003. *Street Life*. Green Linnet Records.

Planxty. 1989. *Cold Blow and Rainy Night*. Original Release: 1974. Shanachie Records.

———. 1990. *The Well Below the Valley*. Original Release: 1973. Shanachie Records.

The Pogues. 1988. *If I Should Fall from Grace with God*. WEA.

Sands, Tommy. 1985. *Singing of the Times*. Spring Records.

Sands, Tommy and Pete Seeger. 1995. *The Heart's a Wonder*. Green Linnet Records.

Sliabh Notes. 2002. *Along Blackwater's Banks*. Ossian Publications.
Tulla Céilí Band. 1996. *A Celebration of 50 Years*. Green Linnet Records.
Tunney, Paddy. 1992. *The Stone Fiddle: Traditional Songs of Ireland*. Green Linnet Records.

Viewing

Bringing It All Back Home. 1991. BBC in association with RTÉ. A five part documentary film series about the history if Irish traditional music up to the present day.

Irish Music and America—A Musical Migration. 1994. Philip King and Nuala O'Connor, Producers. Dublin: Hummingbird Productions.

Lord of the Dance. 1997. Directed by Michael Flatley. Universal Studios. Video and DVD.

The Magic of Irish Set Dancing. 1996. Ossian Publications. A series of nine instructional videos on set dancing with four CDs providing accompanying music.

Mullins, Patrick (Producer). 1993. *From Shore to Shore: Irish Traditional Music in New York City*. Written by Rebecca Miller. New York: The Irish Arts Center.

Riverdance—The Show. 1995. Columbia/Tristar Studios. Video and DVD.

River of Sound. 1995. BBC and RTÉ. Seven part series on contemporary Irish traditional music, presented by Mícheál Ó Súilleabháin.

Organizations and Internet Resources

Claddagh Records, Dublin: www.claddaghrecords.com. Record company founded in 1959. First album: the classic Rí na bPíobairí (King of the Pipers) by Leo Rowsome.

Comhaltas Ceoltóirí Éireann, Monkstown, Co. Dublin: www.comhaltas. com. Organization founded in 1951 to promote and preserve Irish traditional music, song, dance, and language through competitions, recordings, classes, touring artists, and summer schools.

Gael-Linn, Dublin: www.gael-linn.ie. Cultural organization formed in 1953 to promote the Irish language and its heritage through music, song, sports, and courses. Gael-Linn Records started in 1958 to promote and develop Irish traditional music.

Green Linnet Records, Danbury, Connecticut: www.greenlinnet.com. Record company and mail order founded in 1976.

Irish Music Center, John J. Burns Library, Boston College, Chestnut Hill, MA. www.bc.edu/irishmusiccenter. Irish music archive.

Irish Traditional Music Archives, Dublin: www.itma.ie. Largest reference archive and resource center for Irish traditional music, dance, and song in Ireland.

Na Píobairí Uilleann (The Society of Uilleann Pipers), Dublin: www. pipers.ie. A grassroots organization formed in 1968 to promote and encourage the playing of the uilleann pipes and to actively preserve and collect piping music. Archive and classes in piping and set dancing.

Ossian Publications Ltd., Cork: www.Ossian.ie; www.Ossianusa.com. Publishers and distributors of Irish and Scottish music books, CDs, and videos.

Shanachie Entertainment: www.shanachie.com. Record company originally devoted to Irish traditional music, but now includes world musics, reggae, contemporary jazz, and blues.

Song of the Sea, Bar Harbor, Maine: www.songsea.com. Distributors of tin whistles, bagpipes, harps, and other traditional instruments, as well as books and videos about how to play them.

Tara Music, Dublin: www.taramusic.com. Record company and mail order.

www.IRTRAD.com: Irish Traditional Music Website.

www.mustrad.orguk: *Musical Traditions*, online magazine for traditional music.

www.Tradmusic.com: based in Scotland, this website lists concerts, instrument makers, and biographies of artists and has a mail order.

Index

∞

The letter *f* following a page number denotes a figure.